Your Holistically Hot Transformation

Embrace a Healthy Lifestyle Free of Dieting, Confusion and Self-Judgment

MARISSA VICARIO

Marissa's Well-being and Health

Your Holistically Hot Transformation

ISBN: 978-0-692-66240-3

Library of Congress Control Number: 2016906817

Printed in the United States of America

Contents

*For my health coaching clients past
and present who teach and inspire me
every day, especially for Jennifer Sedney
(1986-2013)*

Acknowledgments

Heartfelt thanks and endless gratitude to all my clients past and present who inspire and challenge me to do meaningful work every day.

Also, to the following Holistically Hot Women who without their contributions, support and input this book would not have been written:

Jennifer Barnes

Kara Beussink

Adriana Carillo

Kristina Buller

Kathryn Foreman

April Pastina

Alisa Whitley

Thank you to my editor Douglas Williams and my extended book team, who held my vision for this book, dedicated countless hours and endured many rounds of revisions to make it just right.

A special thank you to Joshua Rosenthal and the Institute for Integrative Nutrition for the movement that changed my life.

To Liz Stein whose guidance and mentorship propelled me forward in my career as a Health Coach and who continues to be an inspiration as an entrepreneur.

Finally, to my loving and supportive husband, David, whose patience, advice and steadfast belief in me keep me moving in the direction of my dreams. Words aren't enough to express my love and appreciation for you.

Foreword

I first met Marissa while I was mentoring incoming students at the Institute for Integrative Nutrition. As a recent graduate of the life-changing program myself, I was eager to give back and help other students on their journey. I instantly felt connected to Marissa's story and her eagerness to trade in her frenzied New York City corporate lifestyle for one that was more balanced, happy and healthy. It was truly amazing to see that Marissa was on a trajectory to change her own life and inspire others to do the same. It's such a pleasure today to see Marissa's dreams and hard work come to fruition with her first book Your Holistically Hot Transformation.

You are what you eat. This has become the backbone of the natural foods company, Purely Elizabeth, which I launched in 2010. As you will see with Marissa's story, food changes everything and that's precisely what we believe at Purely Elizabeth. Marissa encourages starting with what you put in your body, how you take care of yourself and what you believe about yourself. What a perfect summary of how we can all live more inspired and connected lives.

I love Marissa's approach to embracing a healthy lifestyle free of dieting, confusion and self-judgment and I'm certain it will be valuable to so many other women who relate to Marissa's journey and grow from reading this book. With this book, Marissa helps clear the confusion on what it means to live a healthy lifestyle and offers guidance in a fun, relatable way.

I am so proud to see Marissa sharing her message through writing, coaching and speaking. She is sharing invaluable tools for helping every woman find their own version of Holistically Hot.

Elizabeth Stein
Founder & CEO
purely elizabeth.

Introduction

If you're anything like me, you're obsessed with glossy magazines. You know, the ones that come with the promise of sexy flat abs, out-of-this-world orgasms and the secret to knowing how to never eat a French fry or ounce of sugar again?

I used to scour these magazines searching for the secret formula that would turn me into the gorgeous model on the cover. In my mind, her thin thighs meant that surely she had a perfect life complete with a man who adored her, a job she loved and an enviably clean diet.

Everything you need to look and feel your best is within you.

Was I wrong to want these things?

Not at all.

The life you've always craved is within reach.

But was I searching for them in the wrong place – between the pages of a magazine?

Absolutely!

If my years as an Integrative Health and Nutrition Coach have taught me anything, it's that everything I need to look and feel my best is within me, and the life I've always craved is within reach.

I've always felt a strong pull to inspire others to live a healthy life. It's what led me down this career path. Now it's time to share with you my personal secrets for your own Holistically Hot transformation.

Learning how to focus on my own health and well-being changed my life in ways I never dreamed possible:

- I broke out of my dating rut and met my husband.
- I escaped a corporate job that was weighing me down mentally and physically.
- Through my personal and spiritual growth I found the confidence to pursue my dream job as a Health Coach.
- I've cleared my life of negative friendships to surround myself with positive, supportive people.
- I've learned to feel at peace with food and my body in ways I never knew before.

If that's not proof that this stuff works, then I don't know what is!

Here's a little taste of what you'll find inside:

- Tips for stocking a healthy kitchen and my own personal grocery list.
- Simple steps for understanding and reigning in your cravings and tried-and-tested ways to manage sugar addiction.
- Two-minute, feel-good self-care techniques you're probably not using and how to make them a regular part of your day.
- How to make living a healthy lifestyle a habit.
- The secrets to enjoying travel, dining out and spending time with friends who don't share your interests without ruining your waistline or your relationships.
- A handful of fast and foolproof recipes to help you put everything into action.

From Hot Mess to Holistically Hot

In high school, I was a baggy jean-wearing, indie rock-listening vegetarian. While most of the teenagers I knew were experimenting with sex, drugs and alcohol, I locked myself in my bedroom to pull all-nighters. I had my sights set on graduating near the top of my high school class and getting into my first-choice college, Northwestern University, where I would study journalism.

The oldest of three girls, I was born and raised in a secluded suburb of conservative Louisville, Ky. My mom stayed home to try to keep some semblance of normal in our household while my dad, an Emergency Medical Physician, had a schedule that required long night, weekend or holiday shifts.

I didn't learn the phrase "fit out" until I went to Nutrition School, but that's exactly how I felt most of my life because I never quite fit in. I wasn't interested in socializing at high school football games or going to college in-state like many of my classmates. I couldn't wait to leave Kentucky and live in a big city, and that's exactly what I did.

I did get in to my first-choice school, Northwestern University, situated just outside of Chicago, joined a sorority even though I swore I never would, studied hard, and developed a social life. After graduation, I secured an entry-level job as an account executive at a public relations agency in downtown Chicago. For the next three years, I lived in a tiny, yet way-too-expensive studio apartment in the Windy City's Gold Coast neighborhood until New York City and a long-distance relationship summoned me.

I still remember the day I moved to New York City. It was a sticky summer Sunday in 2004. I crammed every single one of my belongings – the entire contents of my 700-square-foot studio apartment – into a U-Haul and prepared for a two-day drive with my then-boyfriend. I didn't know it at the time, but I was about to set out on a trip that would change my life.

We drove 800 miles from everything I had known in Chicago to no idea what I was in for in New York City. Just shy of 25, I was one part lost and another part naïve. What would have been a scary move felt more comfortable because my best friend since elementary school was living two blocks north of me and my then-boyfriend two blocks to the south of what would become my new home, a studio apartment in Manhattan's Murray Hill neighborhood, known for its authentic Indian food and notorious for the influx of post-collegiate frat boys.

This one move would shape my life in ways far beyond my comprehension. My journey to health, happiness and a dream career didn't happen overnight. It has been in the making since that day.

Adjusting to life in a new city was challenging and exciting at the same time. I was working full-time, going to graduate school at New York University part-time in the evenings, trying to establish a new circle of friends and experiencing all the nightlife the city had to offer. About a year in, my best friend moved away for her relationship, and I could feel my own deteriorating with every senseless argument.

Around this time I started feeling lonelier than ever and also unfulfilled by my PR agency job. But I pushed on. I was on a mission and my goals were clear 1) climb the corporate ladder; 2) find a husband. In pursuit of it all, I dated, partied, and worked – a lot. On the outside, my life looked typical of an urban 20-something. On the inside, I was empty.

I went on that way for many years. I completed and defended my Master's thesis on consumer purchase behavior, earned my graduate degree and started a new PR job at a technology start-up. I continued dating and going through the motions both professionally and socially, accepting that this was the way my life would be, yet longing for something else.

I had discovered the sport of triathlon which challenged me in ways I had never known. Running, cycling, and swimming became escapes for me and the gym was like my second home.

***

The summer before my 30th birthday was unforgettable. I achieved two major bucket-list fitness goals that, in my world, put me on the map as a "real" New Yorker: completing the New York City Triathlon and running my first marathon, the New York City Marathon. I was at my peak fitness-wise and after years dating the wrong men, out of nowhere I found myself in an exciting and flourishing relationship, while my new corporate communications job at the tech start-up was taking off. It had taken five years since relocating from Chicago to New York City, but I finally felt like everything was falling into place. My world felt full again.

But seasons changed and so did my circumstances. That fall, things unexpectedly fell apart for me. My job became unstable when the start-up was sold to a Fortune 500 company. Soon after, I went through a heart-wrenching and unexpected breakup initiated by the guy with whom only months earlier I could see a future.

With my family and most friends hundreds of miles away and a dwindling support system of friends who fled to the suburbs or back to hometowns post-marriage or baby, I found solace in food and alcohol.

After-work happy hours turned into hangovers, and my eating habits went from bad to worse when sugar became a stand-in for actual food (cupcakes for dinner, anyone?). Now in survival mode, I was going through the motions by day. Nights and weekends were relegated to sitting motionless and staring at the stark white wall in my studio apartment, sometimes for hours at a time.

One gloomy winter afternoon, as I sat perched on my sofa for hours on end staring at a television that wasn't even on, tears of hopelessness and overwhelm streaming down my face – a scenario that had become painstakingly familiar – I heard a voice loud and clear:

"You can't go on like this."

In that moment, I realized one thing: the messy life I had been living was not the life I came to New York City to live. My life had become a series of recurring patterns and destructive behaviors that *I* was creating. It was the wake-up call that jolted me into self-help mode – I was ready to take control of my life and put it on a new trajectory.

In that moment, I decided I would place a much higher priority on my physical, emotional and mental well-being. When I let everything from there on out be guided by that intention, my entire life changed.

I started by simply cleaning up what I ate.

Until then, my life as a single, professional woman in New York City consisted of after-work Happy Hours, disappointing dates and Girl's Night-Out benders. Dinners ranged from nothing at all or bar food, to mac-n-cheese out of the pan post spin class, to greasy Pad Thai takeout while watching TV late into the night. With a mindset that life was what happened to me, my external circumstances controlled my mood and emotional state, which in turn controlled how I behaved and what I ate.

As a fitness fanatic and junk food vegetarian, I knew it was time to eat better food, so I learned all I could about it and got acquainted with my kitchen in a new way. With cleaner food choices came cleaner and more positive thoughts about who I was meant to be in this world and what I deserved in this lifetime.

I joined a life-coaching group to learn how to change my thoughts and outlook to align with a more spiritual perspective. For the first time in my life, I saw that my inside world creates my outside experience. Last but not least, I finally paid attention to that feeling of nonfulfillment in my career. After five years of living in fear about making a career change, I took a leap of faith, ignoring my family's skepticism, and enrolled in school to become a Health Coach. It was a first step in a new, healthier direction.

Becoming a Health Coach has been the single-biggest decision that catalyzed all the positive changes in my life. It gave my life new meaning and offered me a career where I can truly make a difference. The first time I told this story at a workshop in New York City, I choked up. As I write this now, I still get tears in my eyes. I barely recognize the woman I've described in these pages so far.

While disguised as fun, my destructive party-girl behavior stemmed from the long-held and deep-seeded belief that I wasn't good enough. My self-worth was at an all-time low and even when things were going well, the energy I carried with me didn't support what I was capable of achieving. Looking back, it's not surprising my relationships never worked out, my career became stagnant, and I was too afraid to pursue my heart-centered dream of health coaching. The marathons and triathlons offered a way to hide behind physical achievements, which seemed more attainable than believing I was deserving of a rewarding career or capable of lasting love.

This book is for all the other women like me, to testify that there is a way out. Start with what you put in your body, how you take care of yourself, and what you believe about yourself. That's the Holistically Hot way. Everything you need is within you and the life you crave and deserve is available to you. When you accept that, you can make lasting lifestyle shifts and have anything you desire – a strong, fit and healthy body, lasting weight loss, a career you love, and a loving relationship.

Why I Wrote This Book

The health and wellness industry is at a crossroads. Evidenced by the growing rates of both obesity and eating disorders, women are simultaneously starving and overfeeding themselves, and it goes beyond food.

They're starved for a more meaningful, purpose-driven life and overfed by media messages telling them who and how they should look and be. As a result, they're using food to punish or self-medicate. It's no surprise that, as a gender, our relationship with food has become severely damaged by the habit of facing our fridge or our scale instead of ourselves.

Something needs to change, but the question many women have is where to start and how to do it on a budget of time and/or money.

Every day I turn on the television, open a magazine or read an article on a popular wellness web site touting a new workout, promoting a trendy diet or spouting misinformed advice.

I'm not surprised that I repeatedly hear from women that there's too much information and contradictory health and wellness advice to sift through – it's the #1 complaint I hear. They're confused, misinformed, and pressed for time. I totally get it and that's exactly why I do what I do, so I can help people make sense of it all.

I whole-heartedly believe it doesn't have to be as complicated as we make it. This book is my way of making it clear and simple for those who feel lost, overwhelmed, stuck and confused.

Think of this book as a compilation of the tips, tricks, and truths I've learned in my years of health coaching and studying nutrition. If this book can empower just one woman to feel that she has the knowledge, tools, and motivation to make nutritious choices and take care of herself the best way she knows how, then it has done its job.

How to Use This Book

If there's one thing I want everyone to know, it's that health and wellness doesn't have to be complicated and doesn't need to take a lot of time. Everything I'm sharing with you in this book has my own health-stamp of approval. I'm busy, I've been on a budget, and I've been clueless about cooking and confused about how to fuel my body.

So before you go out and spend more money on the latest, trendiest, all-juice cleanse, or launch into another fad diet hoping for a quick fix, make a date with yourself, soak in the knowledge I'm sharing, and then put it into action in a way that works for you.

The book is designed to deliver healthy habits in a drip-by-drip approach. I recommend you read each chapter and start to implement the tips immediately. Focus on incorporating them into your life for a week or two, then move on to the next chapter and do the same.

Each chapter is meant to build on the previous chapter. I've always believed it's important to understand the "why" behind "what" and "how" so you know the impact these recommendations can have on your health.

You'll notice I touch on high-level science and reference a few studies throughout to explain how things work. I explore how many people unknowingly destroy their health and suggest solutions to some of the most common challenges women face.

Essentially, the book is ordered like this:

- My Holistically Hot ideology.

- How your body works and what keeps it ticking.

- How to fuel your body and what depletes it of energy.

- How to eat mindfully and with intention.

- How to take care of yourself beyond food.

- How healthy living fits into a busy lifestyle.

If you start implementing the recommendations in each chapter, by the end of the book you'll have a life full of new, healthier habits and you'll understand what it takes to effortlessly maintain them.

You can use the calendar at the end of the book to set your own daily goals, but I've filled it in with some ideas to help you get started.

Remember, without action, there can be no change, but don't expect results overnight. There's a method to this, but it's not a rigid diet, so be persistent, consistent and gentle with yourself.

Now let's get busy being Holistically Hot!

Part 1

Holistically Hot Ideology

Angelica Glass Photography

Chapter 1

What Is Holistically Hot?

Since I started my Health Coaching business, Marissa's Well-being and Health, it has been my personal mission to phase the word "skinny" out of health and wellness conversations. I made a promise to myself, my clients, and my social media following long ago that I will never create, promote, or sell anything "skinny," and that's how Holistically Hot was born.

Holistically Hot is a phrase I came up with one day in the throes of inspiration. I wanted to write an eBook that I could offer on my web site that would be equally intriguing and useful. I was tired of all the eat this not that, impossibly intense workouts, diets that eliminated whole food groups, and shakes with artificial ingredients that many health professionals promote for achieving impossible standards of beauty. I wanted to make being healthy, fit and balanced (aka "Hot"), seem less intimidating and more approachable and attainable. After all, I believe anyone can achieve anything they desire.

My approach to wellness is holistic, meaning I look at how every area of your life fits together to make the whole. Sure, that includes food, but it goes well beyond it too. What if, for a moment, we took the focus off food to explore how fulfilled you feel in other areas of your life: How happy you are in your life and in your skin? What hobbies do you have that light you up? Are your finances in order? Is your spiritual life in check? Do your relationships lift you up or drag you down? How is your living situation working for you?

Food + Lifestyle. That's my approach.

When I studied nutrition at the Institute for Integrative Nutrition, I learned there are many aspects of our lives that feed us beyond food. I'll go into more detail about many of them later in the book, but for now, know that Holistically Hot is whatever you want it to mean for you, and it isn't only about food or your external appearance.

Here's what it means to me: taking care of myself and feeling fantastic about how I look and live my life without starvation, juice cleanses, plastic surgery and all that other non-sense.

My Holistically Hot Manifesto, which you can find on the following page, sums it up.

The Holistically Hot Manifesto

Holistically Hot is...

Green salads, smoothies, juices & dark chocolate daily

THE BEST darn ingredients you can get your hands on.

Regular, luxurious **Epsom salt** baths and lavender oil followed by your favorite face mask.

Farmer's market shopping sprees. **Yoga** because you want to. **Rocking sneakers** like you do high heels.

Challenging your body to move in new ways but knowing when to take a day off **Vitamin-D** filled beach get aways followed *by margaritas*

Honest, giggly girlfriend catch-ups over tea, green juice or wine

Becoming **master** of your own body. **Fueling** your body, not starving it **Cooking** at home more than *dining out*

Restricting negativity rather than *food groups.*

The **wisdom** to know what serves & the strength to release what doesn't

Permission to be a *work in progress* rather than perfect

Loving yourself above all else

mwah!
MARISSA'S WELL-BEING AND HEALTH

www.MWAHonline.com

PUT IT INTO ACTION

Spend some time thinking about your reasons for reading this book and set an intention or write a manifesto for your own definition of wellness and what you'd like to accomplish for your health and well-being.

Chapter 2

Why Diets Don't Work

Think of your favorite food, ever. Now imagine I told you that you could never eat that food again. How would you feel? What would happen in your body?

There's a good chance you would become obsessed with that food – even more than you've ever been. You'd probably start to crave it uncontrollably and notice it everywhere you go. And the odds of you being successful never eating that food again? Pretty slim.

This is what happens mentally and physically when you go on a diet. Typically, a diet involves some kind of food restriction or calorie deficit. You might be successful with a diet for a period of time and even see results. But over time, your body will fight back, usually with a revenge binge on the food you were restricting. Diets are a quick fix and aren't meant to be a sustainable, long-term success plan. It's a known fact that 98 percent of people who lose weight on a diet gain it back.

According to eating researcher Traci Mann,[1] dieting causes three main changes in your body that make it very difficult to maintain weight loss. Neurologically, you become more attuned to food to the point where it looks more appetizing than it normally would. Hormone levels shift so that ghrelin, the hormone that makes you hungry, increases and leptin, the hormone that makes you feel full, decreases.

Biologically, your metabolism slows down. So your body learns to function on fewer calories and anything it doesn't use as fuel gets stored as fat.

According to Mann's research, dieting has nothing at all to do with willpower and self-control. Mann's research even went so far as to measure which participants had the qualities attributed to having higher self-control than others via a questionnaire. She found that self-control had no bearing on how well they were able to resist a bowl of potato chips.

Her research is in line with much of what science has discovered about how the brain works. Neuroscientist Darya Rose[2] asserts that when we rely on willpower too frequently throughout the day, it becomes fatigued, like a muscle. Instead, it's better to create habits that automate decision-making. In fact, an estimated 90 percent of our food decisions are a result of habit, proving that willpower isn't a reliable weight loss tool.

Feel better yet?

---

1   https://www.washingtonpost.com/news/wonk/wp/2015/05/04/why-diets-dont-actually-work-according-to-a-researcher-who-has-studied-them-for-decades/

2   http://summertomato.com/use-your-brain-to-lose-weight/

Even more, while a diet *may* help you trim weight – at least at first – what it *can't* do is instill new and permanent habits, teach you how to eat for ultimate energy and prevention, listen to your body, or understand your cravings. If anything, it cultivates an unhealthy relationship with food. The diet culture has exacerbated much of the guilt women tend to feel when it comes to food and eating, and is largely responsible, in my opinion, for the way many people automatically personify foods as "good" and "bad" or pass judgment on themselves as "good" or "bad" for eating certain foods.

In the words of one of my favorite and often controversial TV personalities, entrepreneurs, and natural food chefs, Bethenny Frankel, "food is not your friend and it's not your enemy."

Making permanent changes requires a change in mindset and familiarity with your body, both of which a diet can't deliver.

Calorie-crazed

In the same vein, I want to shed more light on the mistake that is calorie-counting.

I find calorie-counting to be as outdated as smoking on an airplane, yet I'm constantly amazed by how many people still dutifully count their calories. We live in a calorie-crazed world and spend our days adding up the calories we eat, subtracting them from the ones we burn. There are even apps devoted to this crazy-making habit.

I can say that because I did this myself in college. I would lie in bed awake at night unscientifically recalling the calorie count on the elliptical machine that morning, then erroneously estimating the calories I ate that day. I was never happy with the result and I would beat myself up, vowing to do better the next day. It was a dangerous cycle that got me nowhere but onto a therapist's sofa.

If you've ever been berated or criticized by someone you knew, loved, or respected, you know how completely debilitating it can feel. When it happens repeatedly, you understand how damaging it can be. When we beat ourselves up for getting off track by not sticking to a diet, eating too many cookies, or skipping a day at the gym, it has the same injurious affect. After a while, you may even start to subconsciously rebel. It's cyclical and this was my approach before my transformation.

When you come from a place of forgiveness, love, and self-care, a healthy lifestyle no longer seems like a chore, but a gift you give yourself.

This is why calorie counting is one of the first habits I work with my clients to break. Yes, reading food labels is important, mostly to check ingredients. But the most successful eating plans don't hinge on calorie-counting, because when you eat a diet rich in whole foods and low in – or better yet devoid of – packaged foods, calories are far less of a concern. In fact, I would argue that you can eat whole foods – anything that comes from the earth and is not made or farmed in a factory – without worrying about calorie-counting. Instead, you begin listening to what your body needs and understanding hunger and fullness.

Let's break that down a little further. A calorie is a unit of energy and all food contains calories. When you eat, your cells break down food into the smallest units of usable energy. Those molecules get absorbed into the bloodstream and are used to fuel the body with energy to perform daily activities.

When you eat more food than what the body needs for fuel, i.e. too many calories, it relegates the excess food to fat storage, thus resulting in weight gain. This is the basic process of digesting food for fuel regardless of whether it's whole food or processed food.

Let's consider this process in the context of refined sugar. Your body breaks refined sugar down fast into glucose and fructose, the two simple sugars. While they're chemically the same, the body handles them rather differently.

Glucose delivers a quick surge of energy, yet if it's more than what your body can use right away, any excess may convert to fat. Fructose is a different story. Your liver metabolises fructose all at the same time which puts a heavy burden on the liver. When its overburdened by calories from fructose, those excess calories become fat.[3]

Vegetables and whole grains contain glucose. Based on our discussion above about how glucose is metabolized, we know that it's digested a lot more evenly throughout the body. Excess carb calories are stored as glycogen, a form of energy storage, first and the excess is relegated to fat. This is why it's important to not skip meals - so your body can access the energy from your food right away and not store it.

Likewise, we can see how whole foods require more energy to digest (a good thing because digestion itself burns calories) and

---

3   http://authoritynutrition.com/6-reasons-why-a-calorie-is-not-a-calorie/

are used to fuel the body more completely and efficiently than processed foods.[4]

I once witnessed a conversation between two young women: one was holding a zero-calorie diet soda and questioning her colleague who was drinking a 60-calorie coconut water. This example perfectly illustrates the problem with counting calories.

Consuming pure and natural coconut water offers hydration, electrolytes and energy, whereas a diet soda loads you up on nothing but chemicals, artificial sweeteners and caffeine. I would even argue that coconut water can help with managing sweet cravings. In my personal experience, it can help hold me over between meals. Diet soda has the opposite effect – it stimulates appetite and sugar cravings. I'll take the 60-calorie coconut water over the 0-calorie diet soda any day and am confident that I won't gain any weight, even though I chose the higher-calorie option. In the long-run, it will combat any tendency to overeat, rather than spark the brain's chemical triggers that can lead down the sugar aisle.

Similarly, people are uneasy about foods like nuts and avocados that are naturally high in fat. Don't be so quick to write them off though, because your body needs healthy fats to build healthy cells, fuel brain activity, absorb vitamins, and protect your organs. Low-fat cookies or crackers just wouldn't cut it and they're loaded with added sugar and other fillers to make up for the missing fat. Because they're devoid of fat, these foods aren't satiating, so you'll end up eating more to feel satisfied. Moreover, the sugar they often contain will have you craving more.

---

4   http://www.foodandnutritionresearch.net/index.php/fnr/article/view/5144

It all comes down to calorie density,[5] the scientific term for the number of calories per pound of food. Calorie density is lowest for unprocessed plant foods. Filling up on plant foods keeps calorie consumption low, balances blood sugar, "crowds out" unhealthy choices, controls appetite, and minimizes cravings. With this approach, you can eat more food containing fewer calories and potentially create healthy weight loss over the long haul.

If you wanted to fill up more thoroughly and provide your body with adequate nutrition and energy, which would you choose?

---

5   "The Pritikin Principle", The Calorie Density Solution, The Healthy Way to Lose up to 7 Pounds a Week. By Robert Pritikin, Time-Life Books.

1 lb of Oreo cookies with 2,200 calories

OR

1 lb of 2 percent cottage cheese, 2 lbs cantaloupe, 1 lb apples, 1 lb tofu, 1 lb kale, 2 lbs celery, 1 lb lettuce, 1 lb carrots, 1 lb papaya, 1 lb onion, 2 lbs cucumbers for 2,225 calories

Neither option is a real meal, per se, but both add up to the same amount of calories. Let's be real, though. Could you subsist on a pound of Oreos for a day? Likely not, because you'd either end up feeling hungry, tired and moody – or guilty. Because the real food option is fiber-rich, you'll have a more regulated appetite and an even energy output to get through your day feeling more nourished.

> **When you eat whole foods, you can eat more food.**

As I often say, "When you eat whole foods, you can eat more food."

Eating nutrient-dense food fills you up and makes you feel satiated and nourished, and it "crowds out" the less optimal foods you may have craved in the past. Who has room for fast food, junk food and candy when your body is running on real, natural fuel?

You'll begin to lose your taste and appetite for these foods before you know it. What's even better is that you won't even miss them. Many of my clients are surprised to find that healthy eating can be flavorful and delicious, and nutritious food can be fun to buy and prepare. Your palate will open up to a world of new flavors and textures, all of which will have you feeling lighter, vibrant and more energetic.

This book will help you learn how to eat smart and eat well.

There is no quick fix. If you're relying on a pill, a drink, a miracle vitamin, diet, or something similar for your "nutrition" or appetite suppression, you're doing it wrong. Do the work to eat real food. Read ingredients on labels. Learn your body's hunger cues. Know exactly what you're putting into your body. If you feel challenged to do this on your own, invest the money in someone who can help you learn, because your life depends on it.

Freedom from Fad Diets

Paleo, vegan, vegetarian, gluten-free, raw, macrobiotic – it's all enough to make your head spin. What differentiates me from some others in the nutrition industry is that I don't glorify any one way of eating over another. I give my clients a solid understanding of what they're putting into their bodies and give them the tools to understand how their body responds to it. In other words, how it has a direct impact on their health and well-being. Having this understanding gives my clients complete freedom to explore and select what works for them as individuals. While I'm all about putting labels on food (i.e. labeling GMOs), I'm not in any way into diet labels and never will be.

When I first became a Health Coach, I wanted to do a gentle cleanse after the holidays one year to return my system to normal. I decided to try an elimination diet. It was straightforward: Three weeks of clean eating, with no sugar, refined carbohydrates or alcohol, a special broth and some supplements. It sounded easy enough and focused on whole foods. I was in!

I stayed on the cleanse for a week and followed the instructions word-for-word. I felt no different from before. If anything, it was too much food for me and there were times I felt too full or was sipping broth when I wasn't hungry. I also felt completely anti-social when it came to enjoying after-work drinks or dining out with a friend to catch up. I hadn't only eliminated many foods from my life, I had eliminated having fun. The weeks felt long and I couldn't wait for it to be over so I could get back to the healthy eating that I knew.

Don't get me wrong, elimination diets can be useful when guided by a doctor or coach for determining food sensitivity. But by no means are they meant to be a permanent solution, a long-term diet, or quick fix for weight loss.

As the weeks passed, I realized what I must have always known about diets. They can be restrictive and isolating and that's exactly how I felt and exactly how I never want to feel in the name of wellness. What I confirmed for myself and for my health and wellness practice is that I don't condone diets or all-juice cleanses or detoxes. I encourage my clients to explore different ways of eating to find what works for them as individuals. Healthy eating shouldn't feel restrictive.

There are so many diets out there, from Atkins to Paleo to South Beach and more. On my own wellness journey, I've sampled various aspects of different diets to create a way of eating customized to my body, tastes and preferences.

Consider this from two popular books: one advises to cut out all wheat and limit grains and eat very high quantities of animal protein (i.e. meat, fish and eggs), vegetables and healthy fats;

the second recommends limiting animal protein to 20 percent of the meal. Which is right?

Both and neither.

Nutrition is an inexact science. Both of these books can exist because different people thrive on different foods. Neither one is right or better than the other. But, by limiting yourself to a singular set of rules without understanding anything about nutrition or how your body reacts, you could be missing out on an opportunity to discover what's best for you. There's no freedom in that.

If the "diet of the moment" has you wondering if you should conform, consider that how you choose to eat should be a personal decision, one you arrive at via careful consideration and experimentation. I know it can be tempting to want to wrap things up in a neat little bow and stick a tag on it, but life doesn't always work that way. When it comes to nourishment, it's definitely not so cut-and-dried. Would you rather follow someone else's rules, or be free to explore healthy eating and find a way of eating that fits your own personal tastes and preferences?

Take my own story as an example: I declared myself a vegetarian at the age of 13 and quit eating all meat and seafood cold turkey after reading a graphic book about animal slaughter. That choice remained right for me until 12 years later.

Having newly moved to New York City and started training for triathlons, I re-evaluated my vegetarian diet. At the time (probably for lack of knowing how to eat properly as a vegetarian), I decided my triathlon training required additional protein I wasn't getting. Slowly, I added seafood back in. Though

I re-evaluate all the time, that's what's still working for me, albeit for different reasons now. At one point, I even experimented with going completely vegan during the work week. That didn't work out well for me, because my body craved eggs.

However, a few years ago, I decided I would remove all dairy because of some sinus issues. I'm not strict about avoiding it at all costs (except for milk), but I know when I do, I feel better. It's the same with gluten – my digestion is better without it, but I'd rather live a little and enjoy a delicious piece of bread at my favorite restaurant when the occasion allows. I'm just conscious of not diving headfirst into the breadbasket; I savor one piece with olive oil or butter, if it's good quality.

So what is this "diet" I've just described? It's not. It's a way of eating I've devised for my own optimal health, that allows room for a little indulgence here and there – and it's something I arrived at after much education, experimentation, and consideration. I can't see myself ever eating meat again, but if it's something I decide is right for me down the road, I will. I have no shame in that. I like to refer to the way I eat as plant-based because it's heavy on all vegetables and plant foods.

A friend and fellow Health Coach who treats her gastrointestinal issues and controls her symptoms primarily with food, eats to closely resemble a Paleo diet. But that's not the label she gives it. It's simply what works for her and her body.

There are no less than hundreds of "diets," or "ways of eating," out there, but none of them are sustainable because they usually involve restriction and our human nature doesn't like to be told we "can't" have something. Our bodies will rebel every time.

I don't mean to discount those who are strict vegans or gluten-free, for example, who eat the way they do for ethical or serious health reasons. In those cases, the "diet" becomes a way of life. But for the rest of us, I find these diets don't work, especially if you're not fully aligned with your "why," or the reason that connects you to the purpose.

In other words, my experience is that those who adopt these ways of eating for weight loss purposes or to stay "on trend" end up hungry and disappointed without experiencing any real change. They hold themselves to impossible food standards with little to no leeway, and when they violate those rules, they succumb to food guilt and beat themselves up for their missteps. It's a vicious cycle I've seen many times before.

Most people find that combining several different ways of eating, or "leaning" toward a certain way of eating while allowing a little flexibility, is best and most attainable for them.

Ditch the Scale

I used to be an obsessive "weigher," as many women tend to be.

I never really jumped on the dieting bandwagon, but I was constantly jumping on the scale. Every morning at the gym, I would weigh in for the verdict on how I was going to feel about myself that day. That one number – and it fluctuated daily – determined whether I felt "fat" or "thin" for a day.

Client Story: No Scale for a Week

Susan, a prospective client, decribed in detail how she weighed herself every morning, I flashed back to this old habit of mine. She spoke about her daily weigh-ins like she would about brushing her teeth or taking a shower. Every single morning she stepped on the scale. That's what she did for as long as she could remember.

What struck me is how that simple mindless habit of weighing herself every morning shaped her mindset for the rest of the day. It determined how she felt, how she spoke to herself, and even how she reacted to others at work and at home.

I suggested that Susan ditch the scale for a week, maybe two – or even forever – but start with a week and see how different she felt on a daily basis.

When I made this suggestion, I heard Susan breathe a sigh of relief. I had just given her permission to *not* do something she always accepted she was supposed to do.

I recommended she replace the habit of weighing herself with something kinder, like a yoga class (yoga was something she had told me she wanted to be doing more).

If you're a compulsive weigher or scale-obsessed, you should know that the number on the scale doesn't hold much weight.

Not only can your weight fluctuate drastically by the day, even by the hour, but also research has shown that frequent weighing can affect your mood, body image and could be tied to depression.[6]

---

6   http://health.usnews.com/health-news/blogs/eat-run/2013/09/20/
     why-you-shouldnt-weigh-yourself

A lot can influence the number on the scale more than body weight alone.

Your body is made up mostly of water, so its water content fluctuates by the day depending on a variety of factors. Hydration levels, food intake and dietary choices, activity level, and your menstrual cycle all determine how much water you retain. Even water intake alone can cause the number on the scale to rise temporarily.

Carbohydrates are your body's main source of energy. Once eaten, carbs are broken down into smaller units of sugar like glucose, a fuel source for the muscles, tissues, organs and brain. After you've fulfilled your body's immediate needs for fuel, excess carb calories and unused glucose are converted to glycogen for later use. Once glycogen stores are full, any excess is stored as fat. Glycogen stores naturally go up and down at frequent intervals during the day, which also influences the number you see on the scale. Moreover, for every one pound of glycogen stored, your body stores two to three pounds of water.

By volume, fat takes up more space than the same amount of muscle. As your fitness level increases and body fat is replaced by muscle, the number on the scale may not budge, but your clothes may get looser. The scale isn't a real or reliable measure of your overall health and fitness.

Know that your value, capabilities and purpose as a human being add up to something much greater than a number. When you let the scale control your body image and determine your self-worth, you lose sight of your bigger goals and all of the progress and achievements along the way. You become habitually focused on the short term, which can erode your commitment to long-term goals.

Client Story: Dropping the Daily Weigh-in

One of my group coaching clients, Alisa, had been incorporating some of the small changes I've mentioned throughout the book and like most women, weighing herself almost everyday. Then I challenged my group members to ditch the scale. After a month she reported back to me:

"After not weighing myself for a month, I checked in this morning and I was 10 pounds lighter than I expected! I was so skeptical about dropping the daily weigh in, but it's great not to have that stress in my life anymore!"

If you're overly invested in your scale, challenge yourself to weigh yourself less frequently. Start with once a week, then once a month and eventually maybe not at all. Set goals that revolve around making healthy lifestyle changes, rather than those that are focused on a number. Finally, measure your progress by how your clothes fit and, most importantly, how you feel physically and mentally instead.

As I began to feel more in tune with my body and in control of my eating habits, I stopped stepping on the scale. I noticed my mornings felt less stressful and I stopped basing my mood, sex appeal, and self-worth on an arbitrary number.

You are what you eat, not what you weigh.

Detoxing and Cleansing

This is a tricky topic because it's true that our bodies are exposed to an entire range of toxins, from the environment to the food we eat and the medication we take. But I often see detoxing and cleansing used incorrectly as a quick fix for weight loss and that's not the Holistically Hot way. Instead, I encourage detoxing with whole foods and learning to limit the number of toxins you bring into your life, be they from food, people, household cleaners, or beyond.

You are what you eat, not what you weigh.

Now a multi-billion-dollar market, juice cleansing originated thousands of years ago in India as both a spiritual practice and a method of body detoxification for preventative medicine. In fact, most religions traditionally practice some type of cleansing or detoxing ritual. The concept gained newfound popularity in recent years with mainstream marketing and celebrity endorsement.

Post-new year, holidays, vacations, or summer debauchery are all popular times to embark on a juice cleanse, which typically involves avoiding solid food and drinking only fruit and vegetable juices, water and herbal tea for a few days or as long as several weeks.

It's easy to get caught up in a juice cleanse as a quick fix for fast weight loss or as a way to undo eating habits you're not proud of.

Recently, I ran into a friend who told me she had been away with her family and eating lots of fried food, so she was going to do a juice cleanse because she felt gross, had gained a few pounds, and wanted to flush all that food out.

Well, that's not really the way juice cleanses work. In my opinion, juice cleanses can trigger an unhealthy relationship with food beyond any benefits they claim to offer. The purpose of a juice cleanse is to give the digestive system a break and flush toxins out by flooding your body with the enzymes, vitamins and nutrients contained in raw fruit and veggie juice blends. Cleansing devotees experience clearer thinking, weight loss and say that it can kick-start cleaner, healthier eating habits. The results and side effects one experiences can vary depending on the individual.

Many of the bottled green juices sold for the purpose of cleansing contain a lot of fruit and thus have high sugar content, not something you want to consume in large quantities for days at a time. For starters, it spikes and crashes your blood sugar. If this goes on for regular intervals, it can permanently mess with your metabolism and cause crazy sugar cravings.

A few years ago, I was prepared to jump on board and defend my place in the wellness industry as a dutiful juice cleanser. After several failed attempts, marked mostly by ravenous hunger, lightheadedness and a desire for actual solid food, I finally made it through one. Many will say the challenges I experienced are side effects of the body detoxing, but for me, it wasn't worth it. I didn't lose any weight, it didn't cure my sugar cravings, and it didn't help me implement any healthy habits I didn't already have. It only isolated me more than my previous whole-food cleanse. I determined that juice cleansing is not the path to health for me. In recent years, it seems a few others in the wellness community, like celebrity nutritionists Heather Bauer and

Rania Batayneh,[7] have joined me in boycotting the trend. While it's still prevalent, it seems to be losing some traction.

I made a personal decision many years ago that I was finished with trying to live on a steady diet of juice for days at a time and go the route of clean, healthy, solid food for a lifetime.

First and foremost, I liken juice cleanses to crash diets. If you ate too many holiday cookies or partied too hard on vacation, a juice cleanse isn't the go-to quick fix to rectify poor choices. I advocate changing your overall eating habits. This way, even if you go off the rails for a day or two, your body will self-correct by craving whole foods.

Moreover, given clean, healthy, balanced nutrition, the kidneys, colon and liver know how to cleanse themselves naturally and, like super computers, they're quite efficient at it. They don't respond to perceived starvation as punishment.

Many women already harbor a love-hate relationship with food, something I struggled with myself for years. An all-juice cleanse can encourage such an attitude. Explore why you're drawn to juice cleansing in the first place. Are you treating your body poorly otherwise? Do you want to lose weight, constantly feel bloated, or have bad skin breakouts? All of these are symptoms of potentially bigger problems a juice cleanse can't solve long-term.

All diets, ways of eating, and foods affect everyone differently, but for those looking to lose weight on a juice cleanse, know

---

7   http://www.nydailynews.com/life-style/
     juice-fasts-cleansed-sense-article-1.1862531

that what you lose will most likely come back. Weight loss on an all-juice cleanse is mainly water weight and muscle. For long-term weight loss, I recommend adopting healthy, sustainable habits.

The good news is you can reset and cleanse your system with real food, drink green juice and smoothies daily (stick with mostly vegetable ingredients and limit fruit for a lower sugar fix) as part of a healthy diet, and still experience the benefit of a healthy glow, clear skin, less bloating and incredible energy.

Above all, "cleanses" aren't a quick fix for poor eating habits or food guilt. Focus on foods that fuel, and work on changing your relationship with food. This book will show you how!

Juicing vs. Blending

Let's be clear. While I don't condone juice cleanses or fasts, there is a place for fresh vegetable juices and smoothies in a healthy diet. Let's review a few quick differences between juicing and blending and how to know which is best for you.

Juicing extracts the water and nutrients from produce and separates them from the fiber. Blending, on the other hand, leaves no pulp. A blender pulverizes entire pieces of produce to make a smoothie. While the fiber is left behind, blending does break it down slightly, which makes the blended produce easier to digest.

Because the fiber hasn't been removed with juices, it's easier for the body to digest. You can easily absorb 100 percent of the nutrients right away and in large quantities – much larger than if you were to eat the produce whole. Because the liquid is absorbed into the bloodstream so quickly, it's important to be mindful of the impact. If you are juicing fruit, it can cause a rapid spike in blood sugar and unstable blood sugar levels – just like eating candy – which can cause many long-term health problems.

For those with sensitive digestive systems or illnesses that don't allow the body to digest fiber, juicing can be ideal. However, because there is no fiber, juices tend to be less filling. You may be hungry shortly after drinking a juice, so it's a good idea to pair your juices with a fat and/or fiber-rich whole food, like nuts. This is especially helpful if your juice contains fruit, as it slows down the absorption of the sugar.

On the other hand, because smoothies contain fiber, they are absorbed more slowly into the blood stream, delivering a more even release of nutrients and not causing a spike in blood sugar. The fiber also makes them more filling so they can actually serve as a meal – like a breakfast or snack. Finally, blending tends to take less time than juicing and the clean-up is typically faster than cleaning a juicer with its many parts.

Which is better?

It's a personal choice. Try both and see which you prefer. Of course, as I mentioned, if you have digestive troubles or anything that would prevent you from digesting fiber, juicing may be a better option for you. You may decide you like both juices and smoothies, and your hunger level may determine when you choose a juice or smoothie.

If you'd like to make your juices at home rather than buy them from a juice bar, you'll need a juicer.

The **hydraulic press** is a top-of-the-line juicer that extracts juice in two steps. First, the fibers in the raw produce are broken down by cutting, shredding, and grinding until the produce has a mushy consistency. Then the mush is fed through the juicer with extreme pressure to extract the juice and nutrients. A hydraulic press juicer is one of the most efficient juicers because it can extract more of the natural vitamins, minerals, and enzymes than other types of juicers to render nutrient-dense juices with a smooth texture and lots of flavor.

This type of juicer is one of the most time-consuming to use and clean. It's also the most expensive, starting at around $2,500. The Norwalk juicer is the most well-known hydraulic press juicer.

A **centrifugal juicer** uses a fast-spinning metal blade that separates the juice from the flesh with great force. The juice then goes into one container and the pulp into another. One of the drawbacks of a centrifugal juicer is that the fast-spinning metal blade generates heat, which destroys some of the enzymes in the fruits and vegetables. The heat also oxidizes those nutrients, rendering a less -nutritious juice.

Centrifugal juicers start at around $200. Some common brand names are Omega, Breville, Hamilton Beach and Cuisinart.

If you're not too worried about getting the maximum amount of nutrients or you want to save some money, a centrifugal juicer could be a good option for you.

Finally, a **masticating or cold press juicer** is a newer type of juicer – a happy medium between a hydraulic press and centrifugal juicer. The cold press juicer extracts juice by crushing the produce first, then pressing it to get the most juice. These keep more of the nutrients and enzymes intact because there's no heat involved – or at least not as much. The cold press juicer tends to be quiet, but does let some pulp through so the juice isn't always smooth.

These juicers can also start at $200, but expect to spend a little more for a good one. Breville, Hurom and Omgea make cold press or masticating juicers.

If smoothies are more your thing, you'll need a good blender.

A personal or single-serve blender is a good option if you live alone or make only one or two servings of smoothie at a time. You can even drink directly from the blender jar if you don't want to dirty a cup. These are ideal if you don't have much storage or counter space, and you can find relatively inexpensive models. But again, plan to spend more for a better quality blender. Check out NutriBullet, Ninja, and Hamilton Beach.

Smoothie blenders are another option if you make more servings at one time. These have more power so you can easily crush ice and frozen fruit and they usually have different speeds. Most are dishwasher safe and, again, you'll find them at a range of prices. But expect to pay more if you want a quality, powerful model. Oster, Kitchen Aid, Ninja, and Breville all make smoothie blenders.

A commercial blender like Blendtec or Vitamix is another option. These are larger and heavier and are of restaurant quality, so they tend to take up more space. They have very powerful motors and are designed for more than blending – they can chop, grind, puree and even cook food too. If you've ever used one of these, you'll find them enjoyable and not hard to clean either. Of course, they are an investment with price tags starting at $500 and up.

If your budget only allows for a juicer or a blender, go with a blender.

A blender gives you more options. If you really want juice, you can always blend your fruit and vegetables using a little water, then strain the juice away from the pulp with a cheesecloth or nut milk bag. It's messier and takes more time, but it will get the job done. Or you can make your smoothies at home and buy your juices from the juice bar for the time being.

PUT IT INTO ACTION

Vow to release yourself from the rigidity of rules, diets and any restrictive behaviors you may have around food, at least for the time it takes you to read this book. It may not be that easy. If that feels too challenging for you, allow yourself to be an objective observer of the ways in which you may seek a quick-fix or be a victim of a dieting culture.

Part 2

How Your Bod Works

Angelica Glass Photography

Chapter 3

Food is Fuel

It's time to drill down into some of the basics of how things work on the inside.

I'm a firm believer in knowing the mechanics of your body before you start to heal and nourish it. Perhaps not the best analogy, but you wouldn't set out to work on a car engine before understanding its inner workings, so it's imperative you know a little about your body.

Not to worry, though. This won't be a boring science lesson and I won't get too technical or detailed. We'll lift the hood a little and see what's going on inside of your beautiful bod. I promise that once we do this, everything else in this book will make a lot more sense.

Our bodies do more than we realize and we often take that for granted. They keep us breathing and moving and eliminating waste, and we barely have to give it a second thought.

To make it all happen, your body needs fuel and this is where food comes in. Energy in is energy out. And guess what? Food is energy. *So* many women get tripped up when they start counting calories, or categorizing foods as "good" and "bad" – as long as you're putting real food in, you really can't go wrong.

Changing your relationship with food starts here. Regardless of what you've heard or read, eating an avocado won't make you gain weight. If we're ever going to change our relationship with food, we have to stop treating it like the enemy.

> **If we're ever going to change our relationship with food, we have to stop treating it like the enemy.**

So let's get friendlier with food right now and really start to understand it.

There's a lot more to food than how it looks, tastes and smells. Whole foods like fruit, vegetables, grains and proteins are loaded with macronutrients, the main source of calories.

A nutrient is a substance needed for growth, metabolism and other body functions. Macro means we need it in large amounts. There are four sources of calories – protein, fat, carbohydrates and alcohol. The first three – protein, fat and carbohydrates – are macronutrients and your body needs these to function regularly. Alcohol isn't considered a macronutrient, because it's not necessary for survival.

For reference only, here are the calories per gram in each source of calories: 4 each for carbohydrates and protein, 9 for fats, and 7 for alcohol.

Carbohydrates

Carbs, the largest food group in nature, are needed in the largest amounts by the body. They're made of glucose and fiber. Your body converts glucose into energy. The main sources of carbs are vegetables and whole grains.

The other major component of carbohydrates, fiber, is what keeps your bowel movements regular, controls cholesterol, helps maintain weight, and promotes a healthy gut and digestive system. You should be getting a combination of soluble and insoluble fiber. Soluble fiber attracts water and slows digestion. Insoluble fiber adds bulk to stool and helps food pass through the digestive system more quickly. Both are important for a healthy balanced diet in people with healthy, functioning digestive systems. Because different vegetables and whole grains contain soluble and insoluble fiber in varying amounts, it's crucial to eat a variety.

Fat

Traditional nutrition theory divides fat into two groups: saturated and unsaturated fats. Saturated fats are solid at room temperature and most often found in animal products. You've probably been told to limit these and eat low-fat dairy products. I'll come back to this.

Unsaturated fats are plant-based and liquid at room temperature. These are foods like nuts, avocados and olive oil. Finally, there are trans fats, which have largely been banned in restaurants but are found in margarine, vegetable shortening and hydrogenated vegetable oils.

You may have heard the term essential fatty acids. These are Omega 6 and Omega 3 fatty acids. They can't be made in the body and must be obtained from food. Omega 6 fatty acids are mostly found in nuts and seeds, poultry and eggs and lower-quality vegetable oils like corn, sunflower, safflower, and soybean oils, that when heated, release toxic chemicals. Omega 3 fatty acids are less prolific – mostly found in cold water fatty fish like salmon and mackerel, and flax seeds and walnuts. Omega 3 fats sometimes require supplementation. It should be noted that, because of their proliferation in vegetable oils most commonly used in packaged foods like potato chips, Americans are consuming Omega 6 fats in dangerous amounts.

Healthy fats are super-important for overall body and organ function not to mention they absorb vitamins and assimilate the food you eat. Saturated fats, which we're often told to limit or completely omit, are not the problem , according to the school of thought that I follow. However, trans fats found in fast foods and packaged foods are unhealthy and unsafe. Like the vegetable oils previously mentioned, these fats are toxic and we should avoid them at all costs.

You'll find varying schools of thought on this, but according to the Holistically Hot way – and if your body can tolerate dairy products – you can and should eat a variety of healthy saturated and unsaturated fats. The selection ranges from avocados to full-fat dairy products in small amounts like organic butter from raw grass-fed milk, raw nuts, olives, organic extra virgin olive oil for drizzling, and organic coconut oil or ghee, a type of clarified butter, for cooking.

Protein

Proteins are made up of amino acids, some of which your body makes and some it doesn't.

Those it doesn't make, essential amino acids, must be supplied by the diet. Amino acids are used as a source of energy by the body for growth, tissue repair and digestion.

You'll find protein in animal and plant sources. It's completely possible to get enough protein from plants, but it does take some additional work and planning. Everyone needs different amounts of protein so I encourage you to explore how much is right for you.

Vitamins & Minerals

There are fat-soluble (Vitamins A, D, E, and K) and water-soluble vitamins, which include B Vitamins and Vitamin C among an extensive list.

One distinction between water-soluble and fat-soluble vitamins is that water-soluble vitamins aren't stored in the body. They go straight to the bloodstream, meaning your body takes what it needs then excretes the rest. Fat-soluble vitamins dissolve in fat when they're ingested. Again the body uses what it needs then stores the rest for later use. Eating healthy fats helps to absorb these vitamins.

Sugar

In the context of this book, when I refer to sugar, I mean anything that contains fructose. Fructose is addictive and responsible for the many health risks sugar poses from heart disease to dementia.

Sugar, not fat, is the culprit for weight gain. The reason fructose is so troublesome is that it doesn't satiate us the way other foods do. Instead, it makes you want more of it. Most foods trigger appetite hormones that regulate eating. When we've eaten enough, the hormones send a message to the brain that we've had enough and can stop eating. This doesn't happen with fructose, so it essentially goes unregistered by the body. This is why we can eat a lot of fructose-containing foods, like cookies, doughnuts, cakes and pies and never feel full.

Finally, fructose is metabolized by the liver but, again, it's not treated the same upon digestion. Most food is immediately converted to energy. Not fructose; it gets stored as fat.

In addition to weight gain, sugar has an entire resume of side effects and health risks:

- It suppresses the immune system, blocking the white blood cells' ablity to fight infection and increases inflammation, the cause of all disease.

- It disrupts the balance of gut flora, the center of immune function and overall health.

- It lowers mineral levels in the blood, which can cause bone loss, infertility, anemia and irregular heart function.

- It breaks down collagen and causes wrinkles.

- It raises adrenaline levels and causes mood swings, anxiety, hyperactivity, difficulty concentrating, and crankiness.

Sugar substitutes, artificial sweeteners and natural sweeteners must be fine, right? Not at all. These stand-ins don't offer a safety net. Many of them have even more fructose than table sugar itself. The taste of something sweet alone is enough to trigger cravings by setting off the part of the brain responsible for reward and addiction. Manufacturers know how addictive sugar is so they get creative with naming it on labels.

The American Heart Association recommends no more than 6 teaspoons of sugar per day for women – much less than the 30 teaspoons per day the average American consumes.[8]

Choose foods that contain 3-5 percent sugar to ensure sugar intake is kept within the recommended limits. If you're a sugar addict or simply unaware of the sugar content in many foods, this can be difficult to track.

There's a simple way to calculate the amount of sugar in a food:

- Divide grams of sugar by 4.2 to figure out the number of teaspoons in the food.

- Multiply by number of servings in the container.

- If it's a dairy food, the first 4.7 grams of sugar is lactose which is fine, but anything beyond that is added sugar.

- To arrive at the percentage of sugar in a food rather than number of teaspoons, divide the sugar weight by total weight and divide by 100.

Reading labels, not for calories, but for ingredients and sugar content and learning to perform some simple math on the fly can be your ally when it comes to reducing your sugar intake.

A note on natural sweeteners: As I mentioned, natural sweeteners are just as damaging as sugar, and many of them contain more fructose than table sugar. The two exceptions are stevia and brown rice syrup. Stevia is a natural sweetener derived from

---

8   http://www.heart.org/HEARTORG/HealthyLiving/HealthyEating/ Nutrition/By-Any-Other-Name-Its-Still-Sweetener_UCM_437368_Article. jsp#.Vtj--MfFQgM

a plant. It's fructose-free, but 300 times sweeter than regular sugar, so go lightly on it. Many report that it can also have a bitter aftertaste.

Brown rice syrup, also known as rice malt syrup, is another exception. Made from cooked and fermented rice, brown rice syrup is a glucose-maltose blend and also fructose-free. That's not to say that you can go nuts with these sweeteners. Remember, even a sweet taste alone can trigger cravings in the brain, but these are the best substitutes to use for an occasional homemade sweet treat.

The same applies to artificial sweeteners and sugar substitutes like aspartame and sucralose and even sugar alcohols like sorbitol, mannitol, and maltitol (and others ending in 'ol'). These manufactured sweeteners are highly addictive and, while their calorie-free profile may make them attractive, you're better off steering clear. They can rewire the brain chemistry and trick your body into thinking you're eating sugar, which has a negative effect on how your body metabolizes them.

The bottom line on sugar and sweeteners: Don't believe the sugar-free and no added sugar labels on food. Read ingredients and know what to look for.

The Many Identities of Sugar

- Dextrose (and anything ending in "– ose")
- Sugar alcohols (sorbitol, manitol, maltitol – and anything ending in "– ol")
- Dates
- Cane syrup/sugar/crystals
- Corn syrup/sweetener
- Brown sugar
- Date sugar
- Dried cane syrup
- Syrup
- Turbinado sugar
- Agave nectar
- Coconut sugar
- Honey
- Fruit juice concentrates
- Fructose sweetener
- Liquid fructose
- Malt syrup
- Maple syrup
- Molasses
- Raw sugar
- Carbitol (and others ending in "– ol")
- High fructose corn syrup
- Evaporated cane juice
- Maltodextrin
- Brown rice syrup/Rice syrup solids/rice malt syrup
- Diglycerides
- Disaccharides
- Sorghum
- Sucanat
- Glucoamine
- Invert sugar
- Malt sugar (also called rice malt syrup)
- Stevia

Organic & GMO

Finally, since this is an overview of basic nutrition, let's get clear about two terms related to food that may be familiar to you.

Organic food is anything grown using organic farming methods without the use of pesticides or chemical fertilizers. Organic produce can be more expensive, so if you have to pick and choose, you can refer to the Environmental Working Group's Clean 15 and Dirty Dozen guides.[9]

GMOs, or Genetically Modified Organisms, are food that has been altered from its natural state using bioengineering and manufacturing methods. According to the Center for Food Safety, 90 percent of U.S.-grown corn, cotton and soybeans are grown with genetically modified seeds.[10] One of the potential benefits of genetic engineering is the ability to protect crops from extreme weather and troublesome pests, thereby producing more food with a longer shelf life that can be transported to countries without access to enough nutritious food. Other potential benefits include environmental sustainability because GMOs require the use of fewer chemicals, machinery and land, and the ability to improve the vitamin and mineral content of food to fight world hunger and malnutrition.

But for many, the potential risks and harmful side effects outweigh the benefits. Genetic engineering requires the manufacture of proteins not in the original organism, which, when ingested and processed by the human body, can cause allergic reactions, long-term food allergies, autism, reproductive disorders and digestive problems, and even cancer, to name a few.

Moreover, the herbicides used on crops are becoming increasingly toxic and not only harm the environment, they're also associated with birth defects, hormone disruption, cancer and

9   http://www.ewg.org/foodnews/
10   http://www.centerforfoodsafety.org/issues/311/ge-foods/about-ge-foods

sterility.[11] The potential risks are far more extensive than I can cover in this book and in many cases, we're just beginning to learn more. The bottom line from my perspective is that big business and manufacturing are interfering with the natural state of our food to turn a profit and that's not right.

We can make a difference in the future of the food industry and our own health and well-being by choosing to be aware of the quality of food we buy and where it comes from. Currently, there is no U.S. law that requires manufacturers to state that a food contains genetically modified ingredients. The Non-GMO Shopping Guide[12] is a wonderful resource to help you determine the safest foods to buy.

PUT IT INTO ACTION

Take an inventory of the types of foods you eat the most and where you can make adjustments. Too much sugar? Not enough veggies? Short on carbs or healthy fats? Start to get mindful about the foods on your plate. You can use an app to track it if you'd like.

---

11   http://responsibletechnology.org/10-reasons-to-avoid-gmos/
12   http://www.nongmoshoppingguide.com

Chapter 4

Digestion: You Are What You Absorb

Once you've eaten all the beautiful food with its macronutrients, vitamins and minerals, it has to be digested.

Here's a little secret for you: You're only as healthy as your digestive system so you must take care of it well.

Digestion breaks food down into components that your body absorbs. That's the first step, but absorption, the movement of nutrients across the intestinal wall and into the bloodstream, is the next. A healthy digestive system absorbs food properly to use all the nutrients efficiently, which is why we *should* say, "you are what you absorb" rather than what you typically hear, "you are what you eat."

Just because you eat something doesn't necessarily mean you'll absorb it. But if your digestive system is functioning well, you will.

This diagram of the digestive system gives a clear overview of the digestion process.[13]

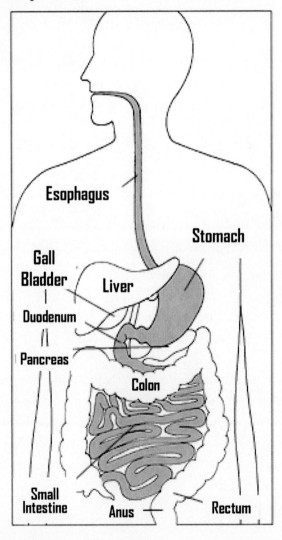

13   https://commons.wikimedia.org/wiki/
      File:Digestive_system_diagram_en.svg

Digestion starts in the mouth and the best way to ensure that you're starting this process off right is to chew your food thoroughly.

Take a moment to think about how you typically eat. A lot of us don't chew food well enough and practically swallow it whole, which wreaks havoc on the digestive system because it has to work overly hard to break down those chunks of food. My little secret is to chew at least 30 times until food becomes liquefied like baby food.

This isn't natural to most people so it takes some practice and concentration. It helps to turn off the TV and other distractions like the computer when you eat so you can really focus on chewing.

I want to stress yet again that this is a lifestyle change: It's not always only about the food we eat, and behavior plays a major role in our overall health. Choosing better food is a part of the Holistically Hot transformation – a big one – but altering the approach to eating that we've likely adopted from our childhood and carried into our adult lives is the other that can greatly impact how your body reacts to and processes food.

How long food takes to digest depends on what you ate, how active you are, your emotional state, and any illnesses you have or medications you take.

The majority of your immune system – about 70 percent of it – is located in and around the digestive tract. So this is why your health can suffer in a variety of surprising ways when your digestion is compromised.

Let's revisit carbs, proteins and fats for a moment. Carbs are broken down more slowly when they're fibrous (vegetables and whole grains) and faster when they're simple and refined (white rice, white flour, white sugar). This is why you'll hear me emphasizing vegetables so often. Because when you fill up on fibrous foods, you'll stay fuller longer.

If you've ever eaten pancakes at a diner, you'll notice that you probably felt hungry an hour later. That's because they don't contain much, if any, fiber and they're usually served with sugary syrup. So the whole meal goes straight to your bloodstream, spikes your blood sugar, after which your blood sugar quickly drops leading to a crash where you may experience hunger, sugar cravings, and tiredness.

Because they aren't water soluble, fats also take longer to digest and require a little more work and the help of some additional enzymes. Proteins, too, take longer and keep you feeling full because those amino acids need to be broken down by hydrochloric acid in the stomach. Once digested, the amino acids are used for tissue repair.

Intestinal Microflora, also called gut flora, are 300-500 species of bacteria that live inside the colon. They thrive on fiber and break down unabsorbed food. This is often referred to as healthy gut bacteria and it's important to keep it that way. When it's thrown off by stress, antibiotics, a poor diet and aging, digestion becomes interrupted, which can cause digestive illnesses like reflux, IBS and IBD.

You can keep your gut flora thriving by eating foods with naturally-occurring probiotics. These include fermented foods like sauerkraut and fermented vegetables, Greek yogurt, full-fat or all-natural coconut yogurt, miso, tempeh (fermented non-GMO soybeans), kombucha, a fermented tea, and kefir, a fermented cow's, sheep's or goat's milk similar to yogurt, but thinner for drinking. Start with a half-cup or 2-ounce serving per day and, as your body gets used to fermented foods, add an additional serving at another meal until you work up to having them at three meals per day or even as snacks.

You'll find that a healthy digestive system is free of gas, bloating and uncomfortable trips to the bathroom. Many annoying symptoms you may regularly experience – anything from headaches to sinuses or bloating – can be a sign of an unhealthy or "leaky" gut.

PUT IT INTO ACTION

Try adding some fermented foods onto your plate at least once a day.

Chapter 5

Immunity: Acid, Alkaline & Inflammation

You may have heard of the term pH in your high school or college chemistry class, but did you ever think you'd hear about it when it comes to your own health?

pH stands for potential of hydrogen and believe it or not, our bodies have one. pH is measured on a scale of 0-14 – 7.3 is the optimal measurement, the perfect balance between alkaline and acidic. It's imperative to achieve the right amount of alkalinity and limit acidity because sustained acidity in the body creates inflammation, the main cause of illness and weak immunity. Every illness is the result of inflammation and we will see, inflammation starts in the gut.

So how can you maintain an alkaline pH?

For the most part, it cdepends on what you eat and how you take care of your body. According to *The pH Miracle: Balance Your Diet Reclaim Your Health* by Robert O. Young and Shelley Redford Young, the right balance of acid and alkaline is maintained by eating 80 percent alkaline foods and 20 percent acidic foods (See chart)[14].

Alkaline foods include vegetables like leafy greens, radishes and cruciferous vegetables like cabbage and Brussels sprouts in addition to citrus fruit, grasses and sprouts, beans and legumes, sea vegetables, green drinks, alkaline water, and Himalayan salt. Raw vegetables tend to be more alkaline than cooked vegetables.

Eat more ⟵————————————————————⟶ **Eat less**

⌐— Can be part of your 20% acid —⌐

HIGHLY ALKALINE	MODERATELY ALKALINE	MILDLY ALKALINE	NEUTRAL/MILDLY ACIDIC	MODERATELY ACIDIC	HIGHLY ACIDIC
pH 9.5 alkaline water	Avocado	Artichokes	Black beans	Fresh/natural juice	Alcohol
	Beetroot	Asparagus	Chickpeas	Ketchup	Coffee/Black tea
	Capsicum	Brussels sprouts	Garbanzos	Mayonnaise	Sweatened fruit
Himalayan salt	Pepper	Kidney beans	Kidney beans	Butter	juice
Grasses	Cabbage	Cauliflower	Seitan	Apple	Cocoa
Cucumber	Celery	Carrot	Cantaloupe	Apricot	Honey
Kale	Collard/Spring	Chives	Currants	Banana	Jam
Kelp	greens	Courgette	Fresh dates	Blackberry	Jelly
Spinach		Zucchini	Nectarine	Blueberry	Mustard
Parsley	Endive	Leeks	Plum	Cranberry	Miso
Broccoli	Garlic	New baby	Sweet cherry	Grapes	Rice syrup
Sprouts (soy,	Ginger	potatoes	Watermelon	Mango	Soy sauce
alfalfa, etc.)	Green beans		Amaranth	Mangosteen	Vinegar
	Lettuce	Peas	Millet	Orange	Yeast
Green drinks	Mustard greens	Rhubarb	Oats/Oatmeal	Peach	Dried fruit
All sprouted	Okra	Swede	Spelts	Papaya	Beef
beans	Onion	Watercress	Soybeans	Pineapple	Chicken
	Radish	Grapefruit	Rice/Soy/Hemp	Strawberry	Eggs
	Red onion	Coconut	protein	Brown rice	Farmed fish
	Rocket/Arugula	Buckwheat		Oats	Pork
	Tomato	Spelt	Freshwater wild	Rye bread	Shellfish
	Lemon	Lentils	fish	Wheat	Cheese
	Lime	Tofu		Wholemeal bread	Dairy
	Butter beans	Other legumes	Rice, soy milk	Wild rice	Artificial
	Soy beans	Goat, almond	Brazil Nuts,	Wholemeal pasta	sweeteners
	White Haricot	milk	pecans, Hazel	Ocean fish	Syrup
	beans		nuts		Mushroom
		Herbs, spices			
	Chia/Salba	Avocado oil	Sunflower oil		
	Quinoa	Olive, Coconut oil	Grapeseed oil		
		Flax oil, Udo's oil			

14   The pH Miracle: Balance Your Diet Reclaim Your Health by Robert O. Young and Shelley Redford Young

Acidic foods include coffee, alcohol, meat and dairy and tropical fruit. Of course, sugar, packaged foods, cigarettes, and drugs promote an acidic environment and are also included in this group, though the 20 percent directive doesn't apply here.

You can test your own pH with a box of pH strips found at the health food store or on Amazon or other online retailers. Follow the simple instructions on the box by urinating on the strip first thing in the morning or wetting it with saliva. Then match the color of the strip to the box insert to find your own pH.

The gut lining is extremely sensitive not only to a poor diet, but also to stress. Chronic stress can compromise the immune system, causing inflammation at the cellular level and a condition known as "leaky gut."

According to the National Institutes of Health, stress affects the gastrointestinal tract by altering the brain-gut connection.[15] Yes, the brain and the gut are linked, practically one in the same. The gut, also known as your second brain, is what experts refer to as the enteric nervous system, or ENS, which is made up of more than 100 million nerve cells. The ENS controls digestion, nutrient absorption and elimination.[16]

A healthy and functioning digestive system acts as a barrier that allows only certain substances to pass through. A leaky gut, also known as intestinal permeability, develops holes that allow larger particles to pass – things like undigested food particles,

---

15   http://www.ncbi.nlm.nih.gov/pubmed/22314561
16   http://www.hopkinsmedicine.org/health/healthy_aging/healthy_body/
      the-brain-gut-connection

bacteria, viruses, toxins and yeast – into the bloodstream causing an immune reaction.

The more this happens, the more inflamed the gastrointestinal tract becomes. The resulting inflammation affects the entire body and can cause anything from bloating, fatigue, digestive problems, headache, weight gain, food sensitivities, skin issues and more. The damage that a leaky gut does to the digestive system makes it difficult to absorb vitamins and nutrients like zinc, iron and B12.[17]

Often, autoimmune reactions in the gut can lead to ongoing and chronic inflammation. Left untreated, inflammation causes anything from wrinkles and osteoarthritis to metabolic diseases like diabetes, cancer, cardiovascular disease and heart failure, neurological diseases like Alzheimer's, Parkinson's and epilepsy, and of course, chronic inflammatory diseases like Crohn's, lupus arthritis, IBD, psoriasis, and COPD (Chronic Obstructive Pulmonary Disease).

To control inflammation, learn to manage stress, consistently get plenty of sleep, eat fermented and anti-inflammatory foods including omega 3 fatty acids, and drastically limit or eliminate sugar, alcohol, processed and fast food and to some extent, gluten. If you have symptoms of a leaky gut, see a functional medicine doctor who can help to treat it with a combination of diet, exercise and stress reduction.

---

17   http://draxe.com/4-steps-to-heal-leaky-gut-and-autoimmune-disease/

Food Allergies, Sensitivities and Intolerance

The most notable and problematic effect of a leaky gut is an immune response to the food particles, bacteria and toxins that pass through the gut lining into the bloodstream. If a leaky gut is left untreated, it can progress into more serious autoimmune disorders. Celiac disease is an example. It is neither a food intolerance, nor an allergy, but an autoimmune disease in which eating gluten can damage the lining of the small intestine, which can be fatal.

Many people confuse the differences between food allergies and food sensitivity, or intolerance. While the symptoms may be the same, the differences can be a matter of life and death.

Food intolerance or sensitivity refers to difficulty digesting certain foods and thus, the digestive system is the source of a food intolerance. Food intolerance is usually caused by an enzyme deficiency or a reaction to either additives or naturally occurring chemicals in food.

If you have a food intolerance, you can usually tolerate a small amount of the food without much trouble, but it's smart to do your best to avoid the offending food to diminish the chance of experiencing the symptoms which can range from headaches, runny nose, brain fog and low energy, bloating, stomach aches or hives. Unlike food allergies, symptoms can take longer to emerge, sometimes up to several days. Dairy and gluten are two common sources of food intolerance.

On the other hand, the immune system is the source of food allergies. In the case of a food allergy, the immune system produces antibodies called IgE (Immunoglobulin E), which invade the cells and cause an allergic reaction. Even a small amount of food, or coming into close contact without ingesting the food, can trigger an allergic reaction. Allergic reactions usually manifest on the skin in the forms of hives or rash, but can also affect the digestive and respiratory systems. Some food allergic reactions can be fatal.[18]

PUT IT INTO ACTION

Test your pH to determine whether you need more alkaline foods in your diet.

---

18   https://www.aaaai.org/Aaaai/media/MediaLibrary/PDF%20Documents/
Libraries/EL-food-allergies-vs-intolerance-patient.pdf

Part 3

Small Changes, Big Shifts

Chapter 6

Finding Your Fuel

When I was 13 years old, I read a graphic and controversial book and declared myself a vegetarian right then and there. My grandfather was a butcher and grocer, so in a nutshell I was shunning the Italian sausage, pork chops, hamburgers and steaks that had always been a staple on our family dinner table. It didn't go over well at first, but I've stayed true to my chosen way of eating ever since. As I mentioned earlier, I've tweaked how I eat slightly over the years to better serve my body.

I have to say, though, I wasn't an exemplary vegetarian – more of a "junk food" vegetarian – a croissant and hot chocolate from the food cart on my way home from the gym, a fast food lunch complete with diet soda, a slice of pizza or mac-n-cheese straight out of the pan for dinner – these choices characterized my diet well into my twenties. Little did I know, I wasn't putting food into my body; it was poison.

One of the biggest and most profound changes I ever made to my diet was to start eating whole, unprocessed foods. I set a budget and would take myself on an early Saturday-morning trip to Whole Foods at the beginning of each month to stock up on basics. I filled my cart to the brim with eggs, fresh fish, fresh and frozen veggies, fruit, brown rice, sweet potatoes, almond milk and more. Then I would replenish throughout the month as needed. I didn't care that I was the only person in the crowded Manhattan grocery store with a large, full cart.

This was *the* way I could manage my food budget and ensure I was prepared with healthy choices at home and at work. Since I had so much fresh food to use, I had no choice but to eat at home and learn how to cook it. I started simply in the kitchen of my studio apartment equipped with hand-me-down pots and pans. and dull cutting knives. I let myself learn and make mistakes.

My first few home-cooked meals consisted of broccoli so over-cooked the green had turned to brown, and I still remember the day I spilled burned rice all over my kitchen floor. My first green smoothie must have taken me a good hour to make because I thought I had to juice my vegetables before adding them to the blender. I had it all wrong, but I didn't let the embarrassing mistakes stop me. Eating healthy food was so important to me that with more time and practice in the kitchen, it became a way of life – my new normal.

After a short period of adjustment that involved some emergency trips to the bathroom as my body adjusted to all the fiber I was giving it, I began to love and crave the foods I was eating. Today, when I eat something processed or of low quality, I can taste the difference because my taste buds and palate have become accustomed to clean, natural, healthy food.

A lot of people think that healthy eating is about how little food and few calories you can eat. But when you choose nutrient-dense, high-energy foods, you can eat more food and don't have to count calories or fat grams.

Because I don't believe in counting calories, I think of food in terms of nutrients and build my meals around lean proteins, lots and lots of vegetables including leafy greens and root vegetables, whole grains, and healthy fats. Remember that a balanced meal or snack should always include fiber, fat and protein.

Make Over Your Plate

If you're going to make being healthy a habit or, rather, a lifestyle, you have to approach it dose by dose, little by little in ways that work for you. Making your health a steadfast, do-whatever-it-takes priority is the only way to successfully create change.

A lot of people wonder where to start when they're first making changes. I say making over your plate is the perfect starting point. Pay attention to the types and quality of foods you're eating, and of course how much.

If you're eating well and making good choices 80 to 90 percent of the time, then you make room for an indulgence 10 to 20 percent of the time. One cookie isn't going to ruin your efforts; just be mindful of addiction vs. indulgence, which I'll touch on later in the book. If you're successful in kicking your sugar addiction, you will likely find cookies are no longer appealing and you won't even want them.

There are two schools of thought on what a healthy plate looks like.

The U.S. Government recommends a plate that looks like this:

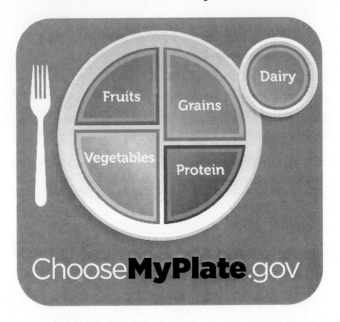

Source: ChooseMyPlate.gov

However, I favor a plate that looks like this:

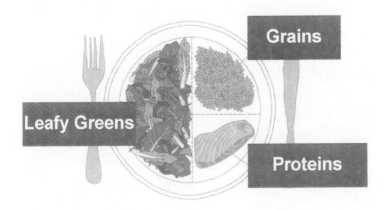

Source: One Medical Group

Let's dig into what comprises this healthy plate of food.

I've said it before but it bears repeating, the most important rule of thumb to keep in mind as you build your meals and snacks is to include a combination of fiber, fat, and protein. It's a blood-sugar-balancing combination that ensures you stay satiated and also balances hormones.

First, I like to emphasize leafy greens and other plant-foods. These should make up half of your plate. Fill it with kale, spinach, Brussels sprouts, arugula, collard greens, broccoli and other leafy green vegetables. You can always have seconds on vegetables.

We're accustomed to making animal foods or protein the biggest part of our meal, but try cutting back on it and determine how much you really need. Four ounces – the size of the palm of your hand, or a quarter of your plate– is usually enough, but if you need more, then have more. Focus on lean, organic, grass-fed and wild-caught proteins or vegan proteins like beans and rice, tempeh, or tofu, if you can tolerate soy. When it comes to protein, the quality of your food is of utmost importance.

Whole grains, like quinoa and amaranth instead of white rice or pasta, starchy vegetables like sweet potatoes instead of plain white potatoes, and any variety of squash as well as legumes like lentils, kidney beans or navy beans, for example, are healthy carbs, or "carbs that count." They provide sustained energy, meaning they take longer to absorb into the bloodstream and won't spike and crash your blood sugar. They're also fiber- and vitamin-rich. These should make up another quarter of your plate.

Finally, healthy fats, which may include full-fat, organic dairy, if you wish, should be an important part of your plate, but in smaller amounts. Think of them like condiments: olive oil drizzled over your vegetables, a handful of nuts as a snack, some cubes of avocado in your salad or in some cases, your protein, like fatty fish, may also double as a serving of healthy fats.

Focus on different textures and a combination of raw and cooked foods. For example, you may want to add some shaved raw radishes or sprouts to top a hot, hearty soup, or throw some cubed cooked sweet potatoes into a green salad.

When you think of fueling your body with food, the following list of foods are the ones that should be making it into your grocery basket week after week.

Top Ten Holistically Hot Foods

1 – Lean Protein: The jury is out on just how much protein is optimal. There has been a big uptick in high protein diets lately. In light of this, it is possible that we're eating too much protein, which can cause high acidity and toxicity in the body. For women, the ideal amount of protein ranges from 45 grams on the low end to 100 grams daily on the high end. I'll let you be the judge of how much your own body needs. If you're very active or pregnant, your protein needs will likely increase. What kind of protein you eat is a matter of personal preference, whether it's seafood, chicken, beef or a vegetarian source like beans or soy.

Here's the bottom line about eating animal protein: it's simply a personal choice, but *everyone* can stand to eat more plants. However, consider this as you make your decision. We've been taught that animal protein is the cornerstone of a healthy diet and necessary for strength and energy. Most quality animal protein is a good source of nutrients, but it also contains some amount of toxins. Even those proteins labeled 'organic' or 'natural' contain toxins, not only from the medication and feeding of animals, but undigested protein buildup in the body causes toxicity. Animal protein also is extremely taxing on the digestive system, which is tasked with breaking down the protein to extract the absorbable nutrients.

Another consideration with animal protein is that much of it is processed, corn-fed, and antibiotic-raised and meat production isn't always environmentally-friendly. It takes more than 2,000 gallons of water to produce one pound of meat. As a protein-obsessed society, we generally eat too much of it. If this resonates with you, I urge you to cut back, eat smaller quantities less frequently, and eat more plants and plant-based protein. See how you feel. When you do eat animal protein, make sure it's the best quality you can afford. Choose wild, antibiotic-free, free-range, and organic proteins to ensure you get the best-quality food. It may cost more, but as your diet changes, you'll need and crave less because other plant-based foods will take up most of the real estate on your plate.

Finally, protein isn't easily converted into glucose, the body's main source of energy. Once your body breaks it down, whatever isn't used for energy or eliminated as waste, builds up in your colon, creating that toxicity I mentioned earlier.

If you decide to consume less animal protein, there are many protein-rich, plant-based foods you can use to supplement. Foods like quinoa, lentils, buckwheat, nuts, hemp seeds, and spirulina are all fantastic sources of protein. Protein powder, a dietary supplement made from processing whey, eggs, soy, rice, peas, or hemp into powder form that can be mixed with water, milk, juice or blended into a smoothie, is fine to use as a supplement if you have trouble meeting your protein needs with whole foods alone. But don't rely on it as a primary source of protein.

WHAT'S IN IT FOR YOU

Protein builds strong bones and muscles and keeps you feeling satiated after a meal by balancing blood sugar and metabolism.

EXPERT TIP

Experiment with how much protein you eat and different sources of protein to find what's optimal for you. Eat smaller amounts of protein throughout the day to meet your protein needs instead of loading up on too much at one meal.

2 – Leafy Green Vegetables: If there's one food that every single person on this planet could eat more, it's leafy greens. They are seriously the best for you and no meal is complete without them.

This is where you get the most bang for your nutritional bucks so load up your plate with them. Vegetables are the easiest foods to digest, provided your digestive system is healthy and functioning properly, making the nutrients most readily available for your body to use as energy. For even easier digestion, blend your veggies into smoothies and soups.

Leafy greens are nutrient-dense and rich in Vitamin K and iron. Spinach is one of the most common green vegetables, but also try kale, Swiss chard, dandelion greens (my favorite!), collard greens, broccoli, mustard greens, arugula, watercress, cauliflower, collard greens and even more. The possibilities are endless!

WHAT'S IN IT FOR YOU

Greens keep your bones strong and healthy for good posture while you're young and prevent osteoporosis as you age. They deliver steady energy and keep your body running like a well-oiled machine so you can power through that 3 p.m. slump.

EXPERT TIP

Add a handful of leafy greens to your morning smoothie for a jolt – sans caffeine.

3 – Root vegetables: There's nothing like naturally sweet root vegetables to add a delicious twist to your meal. Root vegetables grow underground because they're the root of the plant. Choose them during the fall when they're in season. If you have a sweet tooth, eating more of these foods can help curb your cravings and there's something so comforting about them. Go for sweet potatoes, squash, beets, turnips, rutabagas, radishes and onions. These foods have a grounding energy to them, so if you need to buckle down and focus, these are your go-to foods.

WHAT'S IN IT FOR YOU

A double-dose of nutrients! Because they grow underground, root vegetables absorb more vitamins and minerals from the soil. As slow-burning carbs, root veggies are a perfect source of sustained energy.

EXPERT TIP

A root vegetable bake is a simple way to cook in bulk, get a healthy dose of all the flavors of root veggies and use up any leftovers at risk of going bad.

4 – Sea Vegetables: Rich in iodine and nutrients, sea vegetables are natural detoxifiers and promote healthy thyroid function. While they're decidedly less popular than vegetables like kale, sea vegetables are still worth mentioning because they're an under-appreciated and little-known health food that carry loads of nutrition. While they take a little more getting used to, they're wonderful in soups and stews, salads and prepared on their own.

If you're eating in an Asian restaurant, don't pass them up. I love starting my meal with a seaweed salad myself. Try kombu, arame, hijiki, wakame and even Nori, the seaweed you find wrapped around your sushi. It comes in thin, paper-like sheets with perforated strips. Even if you're not making sushi, you can put Nori to use in your own kitchen as a wrap for sandwich ingredients or even leftover grains, proteins, vegetables or salad.

Find sea vegetables in the Asian foods section of your health food store.

WHAT'S IN IT FOR YOU

Smooth, glowing skin, strong nails and cellulite reduction.

EXPERT TIP

Use sea veggies in soups, salads, with whole grains and stir-fry – or just snack on them raw.

5 – Beans & Legumes: Beans are a great, but often overlooked source of protein and fiber. They're also nutrient dense and contain iron and magnesium. If you want to cut back on animal protein, legumes, especially lentils, are an excellent source of plant-based protein.

WHAT'S IN IT FOR YOU

Add beans to your diet and you'll store less fat and feel fuller longer. 2 cups of beans = 25 grams of fiber. 1 cup of lentils = 18 grams of protein.

EXPERT TIP

A lot of people pass on the beans because of their tendency to cause gas. Make them easier to digest by soaking them overnight, or throw a couple pieces of kombu, a sea vegetable (see above), into the water to tenderize your beans as they cook. Short on time? Use canned beans instead. Be sure to rinse them well, check ingredient labels for no added sodium and look for non-BPA cans.

6 – Whole Grains: No, I'm not talking about bread. When I speak about whole grains, I mean the actual whole grain like brown rice, quinoa, millet, buckwheat, and amaranth which cook like rice and have a variety of uses in soups and salads to side dishes and even breakfast porridge. Even though carbs and grains get a bad reputation, for most of us with healthy digestive systems, they're important for sustained energy throughout the day. Rich in fiber and nutrients, including protein, whole grains are the key to sustained energy. All of the ones I've mentioned here are versatile, gluten-free and easy to digest for most.

WHAT'S IN IT FOR YOU

A revved-up, well-fueled workout! How could you resist?

EXPERT TIP

Great news, ladies! Contrary to what you may have heard, whole grain carbohydrates will not cause weight gain! Skip the loaf of bread, but not the whole grains.

7 – Fatty Fish (salmon, sardines, mackerel, trout): An excellent source of lean protein, fatty fish is full of polyunsaturated fats and Omega 3 fatty acids. Grab canned salmon and sardines packed in water for a quick meal over salad.

WHAT'S IN IT FOR YOU

Fatty fish keeps your heart beating so you can enjoy your favorite yoga or spin class, your brain in tip-top shape to tackle a new work challenge, and your skin looking young and clear of breakouts.

EXPERT TIP

When buying fish, choose wild caught instead of farm-raised. Check the handy wallet guide to buying fish from the NRDC (Natural Resources Defense Council).

8 – Healthy fats: Have no fear, healthy fats like nuts and seeds, avocados, coconut and unrefined oils like coconut oil and olive oil are essential to any healthy diet if you want to fully absorb and assimilate the nutrients from your food.

Nuts and seeds are delicious, vitamin-rich and protein-packed snacks. The good fats in nuts keep cholesterol levels at a healthy range and manage your appetite between meals. Great choices are almonds, walnuts, cashews and pumpkin seeds.

Delicious and nutritious, coconut is anti-bacterial, anti-fungal, anti-viral, and a healthy source of saturated fat. It's rich in electrolytes, is alkalizing, and increases energy.

You don't have to go overboard, but do make an effort to eat these foods as they keep you full and can help with sugar cravings. If you're choosing to eat dairy, I always recommend organic full-fat yogurts and cheeses over anything reduced-fat because removing the fat eliminates many of the health-promoting compounds in dairy, including fat-soluble vitamins and in some cases replacing the fat with added sugar, fillers and other artificial ingredients.

WHAT'S IN IT FOR YOU

Recover faster after a day at the beach or an intense workout.

EXPERT TIPS

Look for raw nuts and seeds and avoid anything roasted or salted. Buy young coconuts at the health food store and crack one open (they can do it for you if you ask). Drink the water then scoop out the meat for the ultimate treat.

9 – Berries: Berries (strawberries, blueberries, raspberries and blackberries) are higher in antioxidants and lower in sugar than most other fruit. You can buy fresh or frozen. Antioxidants like Vitamins C, E and Beta Carotene contained in berries fight disease and boost immunity.

WHAT'S IN IT FOR YOU

A strong immune system and a natural way to satisfy that sweet tooth.

EXPERT TIP

Buy berries in bulk at the peak of the season (summer) and freeze them in batches to have fresh berries on hand for smoothies, snacks and oatmeal year-round.

10 – Dark Chocolate: Dark chocolate improves mood by increasing serotonin levels in the brain. It contains magnesium, beneficial for heart health, insomnia, bone density, and hormonal balance. It's high in Vitamin C and electrolytes and contains antioxidants for slowing the aging process and preventing disease. Look for at least 70 percent, but go as high as 80 to 85 percent to minimize the sugar content. Eat a square or two at a time, not an entire bar.

WHAT'S IN IT FOR YOU

Higher spirits + better moods = more love and laughter in your life.

EXPERT TIP

Look for raw, vegan chocolate or dark chocolate with an 80% or higher cacao content.

PUT IT INTO ACTION

If you're not eating these foods, take this list to your nearest supermarket and stock up! Not sure how to prepare them? Choose one ingredient, type it "+ recipe" into Google, and prepare to discover endless possibilities!

Portion Control

I'm often asked about portion control. Here's a little secret: your body should guide you to the right portion sizes for you. The truth is, when you feel nourished and at peace with food, you won't need to eat so much and so often. You'll feel more satisfied from your meals and have fewer cravings.

The cycle of craving and overeating is a result of habitual, suboptimal food choices. Instead of focusing on weight loss and calorie counting, look to nutritionally-dense, whole foods that provide clean, sustainable energy and use your intuition as a guide to controlling portion size.

Portion Size Guide

I don't emphasize portion sizes very often because 100 calories worth of broccoli have a highly different nutritional profile than 100 calories worth of potato chips. In other words, portion size is important for chips – if you choose to eat them – but eat as much broccoli as you want. I promise you can't overdo it; your body won't let you.

However, I do find it helpful to have an idea of what typical portion sizes look like as a reference and so you can adjust as needed. Remember these are typical and not necessarily recommended because when you eat whole foods, you can eat more food.

Size of your fist – 1 serving of vegetables or fruit

Palm of your hand – 1 serving of fish, meat or poultry

Tip of your thumb – 1 serving of peanut butter

Computer mouse – 1 serving of a baked potato

2 fingers – A serving of cheese

Rounded handful – 1 serving of cooked rice or pasta

What about dairy?

For now, dairy doesn't make the list. Sorry, all you cheese lovers! This one's a sticky subject because, while it's not a necessary food group, there can be some redeeming qualities to dairy. But let's start with the not-so-pretty ones: dairy is highly acidic, meaning it causes inflammation in the body. Not only does it not digest well for many people, it can create a lot of mucus, skin rashes, breakouts and other reactions. When I first cut dairy from my diet, a lot of people asked me how I got my calcium.

I understand the concern, but there are many alternative sources of calcium including nuts, leafy greens and sea vegetables. If you rely on dairy as a source of protein, I don't advise it. Try to limit dairy and treat it like a condiment, not a food group.

If you do choose to keep dairy in your diet, stick to full-fat organic cheese, milk and yogurt. If you have access to raw and unprocessed dairy products, give those a try and see how your body responds.

It's worth repearting: Skip the low-fat dairy, which is ultra-processed, unsatisfying and, in some cases such as yogurt, loaded with added sugar to replace the fat. The low-fat versions are designed to leave you craving more, whereas if you stick to full-fat, you'll notice that you're satisfied with much less.

Should You Supplement?

Supplementing is a topic that always enters health and wellness conversations so it's worth mentioning.

I tend to take a conservative approach to supplements and believe that if you're eating a variety of healthy whole foods like all the vegetables and superfoods I've mentioned throughout the book, you can and should be meeting all your nutritional needs with food alone.

However, some people need to supplement for different reasons. In this case, here are a few supplements to consider, but speak to your doctor first:

- **Fish or krill oil:** These are a good source of Omega 3 fatty acids, which also help control inflammation. The two essential omega-3 fatty acids are DHA and EPA – and fish oil contains both. Because the body doesn't make them, they must be obtained in the diet. But most American diets are lacking Omega 3s. Aside from eating cold water, oily fish like wild salmon, sardines, mackerel and black cod, a fish oil supplement is the best way to get enough. Choose a reliable brand that has been independently tested and is free of toxins and heavy metals.

- **Multi-vitamin:** Our soils are nutrient-depleted and some vegetables don't have the levels of nutrients they should. Plus, some of us don't always eat a balanced diet, so this just helps cover all your bases. But these are NOT to be used in place of eating a balanced diet with a variety of healthy food. Speak to your doctor about choosing the right one for you.

- **Probiotics & Enzymes:** These help with digestion and balancing healthy gut bacteria. Look for probiotics with billions of CFUs, or colony forming units. They're found naturally in foods like cultured yogurt (be careful because the added sugar in many yogurts can completely cancel out the probiotic benefits. So opt for full-fat Greek-style yogurt or for a non-dairy option, I like Anita's Creamline Coconut Yogurt, to dodge the sugar), kefir and fermented foods. Enzymes are also helpful for digestion. Digestive enzymes are protein molecules that make digestion more productive and efficient.

- **B12:** B12 is essential for adrenal support, metabolism and maintaining a healthy nervous system. It's most commonly lacking in diets that limit animal foods because it's richest sources are liver, grass-fed beef, milk, sardines, salmon and lamb. Blue-green algae is an ideal vegan source of B12. B12 supplements are difficult to absorb through the stomach, so a sub-lingual tablet can be a better choice or your doctor may recommend injections.

Congratulations! You survived the most scientific yet highly simplified part of the book. It's so important to understand your food and why it's crucial to eat the best food you can get your hands on. This will help you as you make your way through rest of this book.

PUT IT INTO ACTION

Make over your plate by adding nutrient-dense foods into your diet and upgrading your current choices with better-for-you options rather than eliminating whole food groups.

Recipe: Braised Tempeh

Ingredients

- 2 cloves of garlic, minced
- $\frac{1}{6}$ c of mirin (rice wine vinegar)
- $\frac{1}{6}$ c of tamari (soy sauce will do if you don't have tamari)
- $\frac{1}{4}$ c of water
- 1 package tempeh

Directions

1. Mix garlic, mirin, tamari or soy sauce, and water together in a small bowl.

2. Remove tempeh from package and slice lengthwise to create two thin pieces of tempeh.

3. Cut each in half and arrange the slices in a pan.

4. Add the mixture and cover.

5. Cook on low for 20 minutes

6. Turn the tempeh over and cook for another 15-20 minutes. Add more of the tamari mixture if it gets low.

Recipe: Veggie Bake

Ingredients

- A variety of root and other vegetables: beets, Brussels sprouts, onions, potatoes, garlic and carrots.

- 2 Tbsps. olive or coconut oil

- Sea salt and pepper to taste

Directions

1. Preheat the oven to 400 degrees F

2. Dice the veggies into bite-sized pieces

3. Place in a bowl and drizzle with oil, sprinkle with sea salt and pepper

4. Toss to coat

5. Spread on a baking sheet or in a shallow baking dish and bake until soft (about 45 mins.)

PRO TIP

To shorten the cooking time, par boil the vegetables before tossing in oil. Place in a pot and cover with an inch of water, bring to a boil and simmer until the vegetables are soft.

Chapter 7

Carbs that Count

The no-fat craze of the 90s taught us to fear fat, and since then, with every new diet trend comes a new food to eliminate. The latest craze is avoiding grains.

Those who shun grains do so mostly because of their "anti-nutrients," lectin, phytic acid and gluten, a protein found in wheat, which can disrupt digestion and wreak havoc on the gut lining. However, these concerns can be reversed by soaking, sprouting or fermenting grains before cooking. Moreover, many whole grains like quinoa, amaranth and brown rice are naturally gluten free.

Certainly refined grains like white bread, white flour and white rice which have been stripped of the husk, germ and bran – the nutrients that make them whole –have no place in the diet. Even whole grain breads and cereals are processed, not "whole," and should be avoided. But science is split on whether whole grains like brown rice, quinoa, amaranth and millet should be eliminated altogether.

Like dairy and animal protein, you can decide for yourself. My experience shows that if you're a moderately active individual with a healthy digestive system, your body needs some carbohydrates for energy. Which ones and how much depends on a variety of factors and is different for everyone.

Experience and research show that restricting foods your body needs will eventually cause cravings for those foods. So what's my advice to people who tend to shy away from carbs?

Eat carbs that count.

Making carbs count is as easy as being smart about the ones you choose. Some of my favorite nutrient-dense carbohydrates that supply lots of energy and numerous other health benefits, include:

Quinoa
This ancient Incan grain is considered a superfood and is not only a carb but also a complete protein. It's gluten-free and most people find it easy to digest and versatile in a variety of recipes.

Sweet potatoes
A slow-burning carbohydrate, sweet potatoes make a nutritious, anti-oxidant rich snack or side dish. Find a recipe at the end of this chapter.

Legumes

Fiber-rich legumes help stabilize blood sugar and keep you feeling satisfied longer. Lentils are a good choice because ounce for ounce, they're also high in protein. Soaking dried beans and cooking them with spices or sea vegetables makes them easier to digest.

Buckwheat

Not a wheat but a seed, buckwheat is another gluten-free whole grain that contains eight essential amino acids and disease-fighting flavonoids. Buckwheat groats are easily incorporated into sweet or savory dishes. Also check out buckwheat soba noodles for a nutritious pasta alternative, or buckwheat flour as a substitute in baking.

Winter squash

Squash is a starchy vegetable that contains pectins, which reduce inflammation and regulate insulin. All squash is extremely versatile for baking, roasting and pureeing. Spaghetti squash, in particular, makes a nutritious swap for pasta with your favorite sauce or pesto.

Root vegetables

From beets and carrots to turnips and rutabagas, the complex carbs that are naturally sweet-tasting root vegetables can literally save you from your sweet tooth by staving off sugar cravings. They're also the key to a strong immune system, healthy digestion, clear skin and much, much more.

With so many nutritious options, you may think twice about skipping the carbs on your plate and push over the protein to make some room.

Bottom line on carbs: Don't fear carbs! Your body needs them.

PUT IT INTO ACTION

Choose one of the "carbs that count" from the list, add it to your grocery list, and give it a try this week.

Recipe: Sweet Potatoes

Ingredients

- 1 sweet potato, any size
- 1 tsp. coconut oil, melted
- Sea salt to taste
- Sprinkle of cinnamon, optional
- 1 Tbsp chopped walnuts, optional

Directions

1. Cut the sweet potatoes into chunks
2. Steam until tender
3. Drizzle with coconut oil and sprinkle with sea salt
4. Optional: Dust with cinnamon and top with chopped nuts

Chapter 8

Drink Up

Most people – about 75 percent of Americans – are chronically dehydrated – and I used to be one of them! Water is one of the most crucial elements of survival. If you're dehydrated, you simply can't perform at your optimal level. Hydration is the cornerstone of good health. Your body uses water to regulate its temperature, excrete, digest, lubricate joints, and transport nutrients to stay energized.

The truth is, I never realized the importance of water until I started getting debilitating headaches. I drank maybe one or two glasses of water a day – when I worked out. But I wasn't great about drinking more than that. When I started getting the headaches, I experimented with drinking more water. Not only did the headaches go away, I had tons more energy throughout the day and I noticed my appetite was more regulated with far fewer cravings – just by drinking water! It's truly a cure-all!

Beyond natural body functions, hydration is also important for stress management. A dehydrated body has higher levels of cortisol, a stress hormone. Many people also notice an increase in sweet cravings and appetite when they're dehydrated. Thirst is often disguised as hunger.

How much water you should drink depends on your weight, activity level, the altitude at which you live, or if you're pregnant or nursing. It's different for everyone, but as a baseline, start with half your body weight in ounces. If you're running to the bathroom every 5 minutes, it might be too much, so adjust accordingly. A 120 lb. woman should baseline at about 60 ounces. Add 10 ounces more daily if you exercise.

Many people complain that they don't like the taste of water. I get it. I once felt that way too, but I can honestly say that I've learned to love it and my body asks for it. Still, if you struggle with liking water or remembering to drink it, all hope isn't lost. There are a few tricks, which have helped me drink it and enjoy it. I keep a vessel that I love to drink from at my desk and give myself a goal depending on the size of the bottle – i.e. "I need to drink 2 of these today."

If you don't like water, try infusing plain water with fruit or citrus. One of my favorite concoctions is adding lemon, mint and cucumber – it's really detoxifying too.

You can also set a timer as a reminder to drink a glass of water at regular intervals or check out an app called Water Your Body, which makes reaching your water goals each day into a game.

Be sure to drink most of your water in the morning and early afternoon. Drinking too late in the day could keep you up all night visiting the bathroom, which interferes with productive sleep.

Herbal teas and coconut water are also very hydrating and can be used to supplement your water intake, but nothing takes the place of pure, fresh water.

I promise that you will develop a taste for water the more you drink it.

PUT IT INTO ACTION

Track your water intake and if you're not drinking enough, try one of the tips to help you drink more. At a minimum, aim for 8 ounces more than you normally drink, then add on from there until you're meeting your daily requirements.

Client Story: Water, a Well-kept Secret

Kerry is a PR consultant who worked from home. She, too, suffered from terrible headaches that came on almost daily and she also felt an uncontrollable urge to snack all day.

We had tried almost every tactic I know until I asked her one simple question that changed everything: How much water are you drinking? Her answer: practically none. Right then and there I advised her to start drinking water like it was her job (ok, maybe her second job).

The next time we spoke, I was thrilled to hear that her headaches had subsided and she wasn't nearly as hungry as she used to be. Her reaction was truly like she had discovered some well-kept secret, but *it was just water.*

Chapter 9

Superfoods

Above and beyond plant foods are superfoods, ultra-nutritious powerhouse foods that provide energy and nutritional benefits.

If plant foods are the cake – the staples around which you build your meals – superfoods are the icing. Spread and sprinkle them around to enhance your food.

You don't need to go overboard. Try out one new superfood each week or so to get a feel for which ones you like and how to use them.

11 Superfoods to Try

1 – Acai: A bright purple berry from the Brazilian rain forests full of antioxidants, amino acids and healthy fats. Add it in powder form to smoothies and juices for an extra dose of nutrients. You can also buy frozen, unsweetened acai to use in smoothies, or smoothie bowls, a thicker version of a smoothie eaten with a spoon and from a bowl with fruit, nuts and other superfoods sprinkled on top.

2 – Bee pollen: The accumulation of flower pollen, nectar and saliva from bees, bee pollen is high in amino acids, B-complex vitamins, and folic acid. You can sprinkle it on smoothies or in oatmeal. Use not more than ¼ teaspoon if you're new to it and don't exceed more than two Tablespoons per day.

3 – Cacao: This is chocolate in its purest form, not the kind you buy at the candy store. Native to Mexico, the cacao bean is rich in antioxidants, fiber, magnesium, iron, and tryptophan – an instant mood booster. Add cacao to smoothies or use it to make raw chocolate.

4 – Chia Seeds: It's incredible that such a minuscule seed can contain so many health benefits: antioxidants, fiber, calcium, and Omega-3 fatty acids are among them. Add them to your smoothies, salads, yogurt, granola or make my famous chia pudding. (See recipe)

5 – Hemp Seeds: A good source of protein, Omega 6 and Omega 3 fatty acids. Sprinkle these on soups, salads, or oatmeal.

6 – Quinoa: A seed indigenous to South America, quinoa is high in protein but cooks like a grain, and is also a fantastic source of fiber, antioxidants, and other vitamins.

7 – Manuka Honey: A honey from bees that pollinate the Manuka bush native to New Zealand, it promotes healing and fights infection.

8 – Moringa: Ninety-two nutrients and 46 antioxidants make the leaves of the Moringa plant one of the most nutritious plant species. Not to mention it's iron and protein levels are through the roof. Brew the powder into tea or add it to a smoothie.

9 – Spirulina: A microalgae, spirulina is found in fresh and salt water the world over. The complete protein also happens to be one of the richest sources of B vitamins and iron. It helps with digestion and boosts your energy.

10 – Goji Berries: High in protein, amino acids, B vitamins, and vitamin C, goji berries have serious anti-aging properties and strengthen your immune system to fight off colds. Try goji berries in salads, smoothies and trail mix. They can be a little tart on their own. The Chinese believe the fruit can extend life expectancy.

11 – Maca: A root that usually comes in a powder, maca balances hormone levels, helps with infertility, and works with the body's own rhythms for energy and endurance. Add it to smoothies or include it in baked goods or homemade energy bars.

PUT IT INTO ACTION

It seems like everything is a "superfood" these days. Don't let the term fool you or get you sidetracked or confused. You don't have to buy everything all at once. I made that mistake and ended up with a lot of foods that I didn't know how to use. Focus on one or two and experiment with those before moving on to exploring some of the others.

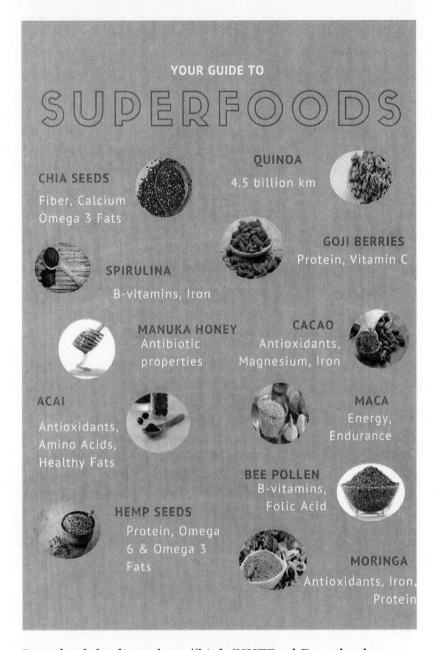

YOUR GUIDE TO

SUPERFOODS

CHIA SEEDS
Fiber, Calcium
Omega 3 Fats

QUINOA
4.5 billion km

GOJI BERRIES
Protein, Vitamin C

SPIRULINA
B-vitamins, Iron

MANUKA HONEY
Antibiotic
properties

CACAO
Antioxidants,
Magnesium, Iron

ACAI
Antioxidants,
Amino Acids,
Healthy Fats

MACA
Energy,
Endurance

BEE POLLEN
B-vitamins,
Folic Acid

HEMP SEEDS
Protein, Omega
6 & Omega 3
Fats

MORINGA
Antioxidants, Iron,
Protein

Download this list at http://bit.ly/HHTBookDownloads

Recipe: Chia Seed Pudding

The secret to making good chia pudding is getting the right ratio of chia seeds to liquid. I've already figured this out for you.

Ingredients

- ¼ cup chia seeds
- 1 ½ cups unsweetened, non-dairy milk (I prefer coconut milk)
- drizzle of brown rice syrup (optional)

Directions

1. Combine chia seeds and milk in a glass jar, like a mason jar.

2. Cover the mixture tightly with a lid and shake well.

3. Put it in the refrigerator and let it sit overnight.

4. Shake it one or two more times before you go to sleep to make sure the seeds don't stick together , especially at the bottom.

Part 4

Cooking at Home

Benjamin Chasteen/Epoch Times

Chapter 10

Simple Techniques for Simple Food

I'm from an Italian family, so my mom and grandmothers have practically spent their lives cooking. Home-cooked food was a part of my upbringing. You'd think I would know my way around a kitchen. My sisters certainly do. But I used to joke that the cooking gene missed me.

Most people don't believe me when I tell them that until six years ago, I had never set foot in a kitchen. Mac and cheese and slice-and-bake cookies were my staples, but mostly I would make do with a deli salad for lunch and settle on a cringe-worthy dinner of pizza, cheese and crackers, or canned soup. I was definitely NOT a good cook. But my desire to eat healthier was so strong that I just got down to business and taught myself how to do it.

Before that point, I had convinced myself I was too busy with work and social events to cook and, besides, I was single. The real fear was that I had no idea what to do or where to start.

When I started to clean up my eating with wholesome, healthful food, I began to take an interest in cooking. Now I teach sold-out cooking classes in New York City to inspire others to get into their kitchen and cook!

When I changed my eating habits, it became very clear, very fast that I needed to figure out the whole cooking thing. At the time, I was convinced healthy food had no flavor so I just steamed and grilled and microwaved sans seasonings and ate a lot of plain-tasting foods.

From the beginning, my approach has been simple techniques for simple food. This makes the task of cooking much easier to digest.

But I love food and before long I was craving flavor. Somewhere between then and now I taught myself how to make healthy food taste impressively gourmet. If I can do it, anyone can and you'll be surprised to know that it doesn't take hours in the kitchen to make it happen, just a little know-how.

My simple food prep also meant I kept my kitchen gadgets simple too, with items like a rice cooker and steam basket.

From the beginning, my approach has been simple techniques for simple food. This makes the task of cooking much easier to digest.

What I love most about cooking at home is that I know exactly what's in my food.

Home-cooked food is much easier to digest and I feel happier and more peaceful eating it because I know it was made with love and intention. When I consistently cook at home, the cost savings have shown.

Sure, I've had some trials and tribulations along the way. Like the time I called my mom in tears, hands emblazoned in red and burning with pain, after chopping several varieties of peppers for fresh salsa. Lesson learned: wear gloves. And I've had to get creative with some of the cramped wall space landlords have tried to pass off as kitchens i.e. mixing healthy brownie batter on the sofa.

But I've also had some grand successes. My delicious and nutritious Dr. Oz-approved Chia Pancakes come to mind! I created these pancakes for my appearance on the Dr. Oz Show. Of course, they required a couple of failed attempts before perfecting a recipe that would impress Dr. Oz, but what I've learned along the way is that the kitchen can be a playground and it's the trial and error aspect of cooking and baking that make it such a creative outlet and a welcome escape for me.

Cooking at home is one of the best things you can do for your health because you know exactly what you're putting in your food. Restaurants are known for their extra-large serving sizes and you can't always be sure about the quality of the ingredients.

A study referenced in the December 2012 issue of *Whole Living Magazine* found that those trying to lose weight lost 5 pounds more when they cooked at home than those who relied on food from restaurants.

PUT IT INTO ACTION

The best way to cook at home more often is to plan for it. Every Sunday, survey your week and decide on which days you'll eat at home. Commit to those days and plan your meals ahead of time so you'll have all the ingredients you'll need on hand. If you can prep anything to make it easier, do that too.

A Note on Microwaves

Reheating leftovers in the microwave seems simple and harmless, but for a long time researchers thought microwaving was dangerous and harmful. Microwaves transmit electromagnetic energy that gives off radiation used to heat food by a process of molecular friction. The theory was that in doing so, it changed the molecular structure of the food and destroyed its nutritional value.

However, new research from Harvard says otherwise. It places the microwave at the top of the list of nutritionally sound ways to cook vegetables and retain most of the nutrients because it can heat food for a short amount of time with little liquid, in essence steaming the food from the inside out. The stovetop can do the same.

Still, it's worth being careful with microwaves. Don't reheat food in plastic containers and replaced rusted microwaves which can be an indication of radiation leakage.

Whether you choose to use a microwave is a personal choice, but I advocate getting familiar with your stove and natural heat sources to cook your food.

Recipe: Oz-approved Chia Pancakes

Makes 12 pancakes

Ingredients

- 1 cup gluten-free oats
- ¼ cup almond meal
- ¼ cup ground chia
- ¼ cup shredded unsweetened coconut
- 1 ½ bananas, mashed
- 2 eggs (or use 2 tbsp ground chia mixed with 6 tbsp water)
- 1 tsp baking powder
- 1 pinch of sea salt
- 1 tbsp coconut oil
- 1 ¼ cup almond milk
- 2 dashes cinnamon
- 1 tsp vanilla extract

For topping

- Toasted pecans

- Sliced banana

- Whole chia seeds

- Ground cinnamon

- Maple syrup

Directions

1. Add all ingredients, except the toppings and the bananas, to a blender. Blend until smooth, then add bananas and blend again. Heat a skillet and grease with coconut oil.

2. Pour batter onto the skillet in uniform circles and wait for them to bubble.

3. Flip and cook until golden brown on both sides.

4. Top with toasted pecans, sliced bananas, cinnamon, chia seeds and pure maple syrup.

Chapter 11

Stocking a Healthy Kitchen

My guide to stocking a healthy kitchen is a simple list of ingredients and gadgets you'll need to whip up a meal as impressive as it is healthy, all at a moment's notice. Say goodbye to takeout and frozen meals and welcome more energy and smaller waistlines.

Cooking Essentials

Now that we've established how much I love being in the kitchen, it's time to prove to you that creating a healthy and tasty meal can be simple and surprise – it isn't a complete time suck either.

If you want to get control of your health and feel good consistently, you must eat at home more often than you dine out.

If you want to get control of your health and feel good consistently, you must eat at home more often than you dine out.

For those who find their kitchen as intimidating and unapproachable as the High School Football Captain, let me help you get started.

Part of living a healthier lifestyle is being prepared with everything you need to make it happen. Stocking a healthy kitchen isn't complicated or expensive. Many people let not having a perfect kitchen or a ton of fancy utensils stop them from cooking. Please don't let those minor details hold you back!

You don't need a lot of expensive tools to create a healthy meal. As I've said before, I started eating healthier in my studio apartment with some hand-me-down pots and pans and a cheap plastic blender – like the ones you used to make frozen margaritas in college. I also had a steam basket, a George Foreman Grill and some dull cutting knives – that's about it.

The more I cooked, the more I added and I'm still adding new utensils all the time. But truth be told, I most often use the simple basics.

Let me introduce to you five inexpensive kitchen cooking essentials that make everything a lot easier.

1 – Blender: I'll be the first to tell you that you don't have to break the bank on a powerful, high quality blender. Get the best one you can afford and use it to mix up smoothies, nut milks, salad dressings, soups and more!

2 – Chef's Knife: Whether you choose a heavier German model, a lighter Japanese one or a hybrid, this item will be a bit more of an investment. The good news is you don't need an entire block of knives. Just one or two good chef's knives will do the trick. Try a few out and choose the one that feels best in your hand. A good knife will make the task of chopping up veggies more enjoyable and a lot speedier.

3 – Microplane Zester: A long, slender metal grater on a handle, professional chefs sing the praises of these things. They zest or grate anything from citrus to fresh, whole spices and even garlic, and are the perfect way to add finishing flavors to anything you make.

4 – Mandoline: I don't know how I ever lived without one of these. A mandolin is a flat frame with a metal cutting blade used for slicing vegetables. You basically run the vegetable over the blade. It offers a quick way to throw together a salad or thinly slice difficult-to-cut root veggies like beets, sweet potatoes and fennel. I even use it to quickly slice onions so my eyes don't water!

5 – Steam Basket: This is one of the first cooking tools I ever owned. For the first year I spent learning how to cook, I steamed every single vegetable imaginable. And truth be told, when I'm feeling time-crunched in the kitchen, I still do. Steam baskets come in a variety of forms. The stainless steel fold-up variety fits inside a pot to keep the vegetables above water. Some pots are specifically made with holes in the bottom for steaming over another pot of water. These aren't expensive. You may want to invest in a few different kinds.

And of course you need a good set of pots and pans. Be careful with non-stick because they're treated with harmful chemicals that seep into your food. Pots and pans come in many varieties, from copper to cast iron, but if you're just starting out, the best all-purpose cookware is stainless steel. All-clad is a good option if you can spend more money. This stuff lasts so don't be afraid to make a small investment if it's in your budget.

With these five tools, a few pots and pans and a handful of healthy recipes, you'll be on your way to healthy meals in no time, but if you want to take it a step further, consider investing in a food processor. I love my food processor because I can process a bag of shredded coconut into coconut butter, or raw almonds into almond butter. Of course, a high powered blender can do the same, but my food processor allows me to shred zucchini for making gluten-free breads with hidden veggies or shred carrots or broccoli stems for a stir fry.

It's nice to have the option between the two. I tend to gravitate to my food processor for veggie prep for the breads and stir fry and use my blender for blended veggie soups and smoothies.

Finally, a spiralizer is a tool with interchangeable blades and a hand crank used to turn vegetables like zucchini, squash and sweet potatoes into shapes that can be used as a substitute for noodles. Spiralizers are inexpensive and a fun way to add even more vegetables into your meals in creative ways.

Pantry Essentials

Likewise, if you think making a home-cooked meal means a time-consuming trip to the store, expensive ingredients, and slaving over a stove – all after a long day at the office – think again. With the onslaught of grocery delivery services available, you can shop from home or work. And think about this: dining out or food delivery will cost you about $15 per meal (and that's being conservative). For $15 - $20 worth of ingredients, you can cook once and eat two or three times with leftovers. Dining out or getting food delivery can cost up to twice as much.

You also won't need fancy storage containers. Mason jars are cute, inexpensive and work great to keep nuts, seeds and whole grains fresh. I store them on the counter top away from light and heat or in my refrigerator to extend their shelf life.

Take a peek at my shopping list. These are the many items you'll find in my pantry at home on any given week and no, not all at the same time! When we get to meal planning, I'll let you in on how to know what to buy and when so you're not aimlessly buying a cartload of ingredients without a plan to use them.

Sample Shopping List

- ☑ **Garlic, onion and ginger:** Used together or alone, these meal starters are best in stir fry, sauces, and salad dressings. As an added bonus, they contain anti-inflammatory properties and fight infection.

- ☑ **Lemons and Limes:** Add zing to salads, fish, vegetables, salad dressings, and plain water. Citrus alkalizes the blood, aids digestion, and promotes weight loss.

- ☑ **Tahini:** A savory paste made from sesame seeds, tahini is ideal for dips and spreads, sauces, and salad dressings.

- ☑ **Miso:** Versatile in recipes and a good source of B12 for vegans, the fermented soybean paste has a salty taste and buttery texture making it perfect as a soup stock, a sandwich spread, a marinade, or a key ingredient in Asian-inspired salad dressing.

- ☑ **Tamari:** Another fermented soy food, tamari is similar to soy sauce and can be purchased without wheat ingredients for those with gluten sensitivity. Use tamari in place of salt for seasoning food and for sautéing vegetables. Fermented foods act as digestive aids.

☑ **Apple Cider Vinegar:** This tart condiment cleanses the digestive tract and increases circulation. It can be taken by the spoonful, or reap its benefits by using it in salad dressings and sauces.

☑ **Nut and Seed Butters:** Use all-natural nut and seed butters to add healthy fats to your diet. Try almond, cashew, walnut, macadamia nut and sunflower seed butters. For a healthy snack, spread them onto rice cakes, sprouted grain or gluten-free bread, or scoop into smoothies.

☑ **Whole grains:** Keep whole grains like brown rice, quinoa, or millet at the ready because they provide sustained energy and plenty of vitamins. Reheat whole grains as a breakfast porridge with milk, chopped nuts, cinnamon and fresh or dried fruit, add them cold to green salads or make your own grain salad with chopped nuts, dried fruit, herbs, and vinaigrette. You can buy them in bulk and store them in glass mason jars on the counter top. Keep a few different types on hand and feel free to mix and match them when you cook.

☑ **Vegetables and Leafy Greens:** As you know by now, these are the #1 most important food you can eat. Eat them daily and eat them often. They're great blood purifiers and detoxifiers, key for disease prevention and immune system boosters.

Keep a bunch of your favorite leafy greens on hand for vital energy and blend into juices, smoothies, salads and stir fry. Rotate your greens and try a new kind each time you shop and remember to select what's in season.

☑ **Beans:** Canned or dried, beans are an often-overlooked source of protein as well as fiber, iron, and folic acid. Serve with whole grains for a complete protein, add them to soups or salads and blend them with seasoning for dips. I love lentils, pinto beans, black beans, and cannellini beans. For dried beans, you'll need to soak them before cooking to make them easier to digest.

☑ **Milk and dairy alternatives:** Whether your preference is cow's, goat's, sheep's, soy, or nut-or grain-based dairy alternatives, they are easily incorporated into snacks, breakfasts, lunches, dinners and healthy desserts. Buy unsweetened or make them at home to completely avoid all additives. You can find a video of me making nut milk at http://bit.ly/NutMilkVideo.

☑ **Tempeh:** Vegans and vegetarians alike will delight in this fermented soybean cake with a nutty flavor that can be marinated, sautéed, braised, or grilled and added to soups, casseroles, stir fry and atop salads.

☑ **Nori:** An edible seaweed best known for its use in sushi, Nori is sold in thin, paper-like sheets and packed full of minerals that beautify skin, hair and nails. Toast nori sheets by passing them over an open flame and use as a wrap for leftover cooked vegetables and whole grains or stuff with your favorite salad ingredients.

☑ **Natural Sweeteners:** Use caution with natural sweeteners like honey, agave nectar and coconut sugar, as many are just as addictive and unhealthy as table sugar. Go for fructose-free natural sweeteners like stevia and brown rice syrup, which won't spike your blood sugar the way others will. Like any sweet food, use them in moderation.

☑ **Herbal Tea:** This centuries-old hot drink can set the mood, curb cravings, and prevent disease. Start your day with green tea, end your meal with peppermint tea; fight cravings with licorice tea and unwind with chamomile.

☑ **Fresh and dried herbs:** Herbs are the perfect way to naturally season your food without added salt. Try different ones and extend the life of fresh herbs by storing them in the fridge in a few inches of water, as you would flowers. You can also buy dried seasonings in a jar to keep on hand in your spice cabinet, but fresh herbs have a brighter flavor and less is always more. consider basil, bay leaf, cumin, dill, thyme, garlic, oregano, rosemary, and sage. You can also grow your own herbs on your windowsill for pennies to use as needed.

PRO TIP

Worried you bought too many herbs or greens and are afraid they'll go bad? Stash them in the freezer to use as needed. Travel a lot or work late? Buy frozen veggies to ensure you have eats always on hand for a quick healthy meal.

☑ **Sprouts:** These superfoods that look like weeds are too often forgotten when it comes to healthy eating. Sprouts have up to 100 times more enzymes than raw fruits and vegetables and they have lots of protein and fiber. The sprouting process makes the calcium and magnesium more bioavailable, not to mention sprouts are antioxidants and have an alkalizing effect on the body to prevent inflammation.

Many grocery stores sell sprouts and you'll find them at the farmer's market in the spring especially. Some varieties to look for include: broccoli sprouts, clover sprouts, lentil sprouts, radish sprouts, mung bean, pea shoots, wheat grass, alfalfa, and sunflower sprouts. Some have a milder flavor while others are spicy. Add them to salads, top soups or blend into smoothies. Try them out and see what you think.

☑ **Nuts & Seeds:** Available in bulk or packaged. I recommend raw and unsalted or sprouted for the most nutrition. Try different kinds, make a trail mix, process into nut butters, or make your own nut milks.

☑ **Spices & condiments:**– Enhance the flavor and aroma of food with spices that can also help digestion, tenderize food, warm or cool the body or curb sweet cravings. Spices can be picked up as you need them for recipes or you can purchase a new one every couple of weeks. Pretty soon you'll have a full spice rack. Some that I use frequently: cayenne pepper, turmeric, cinnamon, sea salt and black pepper and cumin.

Condiments are a healthy way to add flavor to food and are helpful when making your own salad dressings and sauces (goodbye bottled stuff!) There are tons to try but a few of my staples include: Tahini, tamari (a wheat-free soy sauce), apple cider vinegar, hot sauce, dulse flakes (dulse is a sea vegetable), raw local honey, local maple syrup, and gomasio (a combination of unhulled sesame seeds and sea salt that can be sprinkled over whole grains or steamed vegetables).

☑ **Oils:** High quality, organic oils are another good source of healthy fat. Keep a variety of oils around – coconut and grape seed oil for high heat cooking, olive oil for medium heat sautéing, and toasted sesame and flax oil for drizzling on salads, vegetables and whole grains before serving (olive oil is also good for this). Always look for unrefined oils to ensure the best quality.

You'll begin to notice that a lot of your favorite healthy recipes will call for some of these ingredients time and again, so don't worry about buying something and using it once. That's unlikely.

Simple Food Prep Methods and Healthy Shortcuts

Recipes are wonderful for when you want to feel prepared, but I'm here to tell you that you don't always *NEED* a recipe to whip up a healthy meal. Sometimes you'll get all your gorgeous fresh veggies home and you'll be like, ok what next? Here are a few of my go-to cooking methods for when I'm feeling uninspired, pressed for time or at a loss in the kitchen. The result is always something delicious and enjoyable.

Steaming is a surefire way to prepare simple, clean-tasting vegetables, without salt, oil or seasoning. It's especially helpful when you're just starting out so you can get to know how vegetables taste in their most simple, pure form. Steaming takes 5-10 minutes for green leafy vegetables, and 10-25 minutes for roots. All you need is a steam basket and a pot with a lid filled with about two inches of water.

There are a number of ways to make plain steamed vegetables more exciting. Some ideas are adding olive oil and lemon or toasted sesame oil, seasoning the steaming water, or sprinkling the steamed vegetables with herbs.

Blanching, or quick boiling, is another way to prepare vegetables quickly and "cleanly." Blanching breaks down the vegetables' fiber fast, more so than steaming, which can make them easier to digest. Blanching vegetables also removes the raw flavor and brightens up their color. Blanched veggies are always impressive on a crudité.

Sprouting is the process of soaking foods to be eaten raw or cooked. You can sprout anything yourself at home, including beans, nuts seeds and grains and it's easy to do. While not a cooking method, it prepares foods that can be difficult to digest on their own for cooking or raw preparation by removing any anti-nutritional compounds and proteins. When you soak these foods (use a 1:1 ratio of water to the food you're sprouting), you'll see small sprouts begin to form. This is the same process that creates the sprouts you eat (see the above shopping list), but in this case we're not doing it to produce more food, just to make the nutrients in the foods we're working with more bioavailable and easier on our digestive system.

Stir-frying is a quick and nutritious way to prepare vegetables. You can stir-fry in oil or in water. Stir-frying in oil makes a tastier dish since the hot oil seals in the flavor. You can use any kind of vegetables. The softer vegetables like Chinese cabbage, bok choy, thinly sliced carrots, mushrooms, red, yellow or orange peppers, and onions will only take a few minutes to cook.

Baking brings out the sweet essence of the vegetables. Many vegetables like squash and roots taste best when baked. While cooking vegetables this way takes a little longer, it's worth it. If you want to speed up the baking time, par boil the vegetables by submerging them in boiling water first until they soften.

One of the common challenges I hear from clients is that they don't have time to prepare and eat healthy food. Instead, they opt for takeout or skipping meals altogether. I used to think like that, too. But the moment I woke up to the fact that food is fuel, and the quality of the energy I put into my body is the quality of the energy I'll get out, it was easy to change my eating habits.

The problem: The pace of my life didn't lend itself to spending hours in the kitchen. So I dug in, researched and tested, and came up with a set of easy hacks for making great-tasting nutritious food – fast.

Next time you catch yourself thinking healthy has to mean complicated, put one of these hacks into action.

Turn Your Fridge into a Salad Bar: One of the biggest appeals of salad bars is the crisp veggies that are laid out and cut up. You can do the exact same thing – in your refrigerator. When you get your groceries home, slice and dice your produce right away (if you're really short on time, many grocery stores offer pre-cut vegetables though they often have a higher price tag), then store it in individual stay-fresh containers. When you have no plan, you can always throw together a big salad. Just pull everything out of the fridge, assemble your meal, and put it all back where you found it.

Pre-assemble Your Smoothie: Even something as simple as a smoothie can become daunting when you're punching a clock to get out the door in the morning. The solution? Layer all your ingredients in your blender bottle the night before (you can even add the liquid if you'd like) and store in the fridge. In the morning, take the bottle out, add ice, blend it up, and grab a straw. You've got a delicious and nourishing smoothie-to-go in seconds. *Or*, prepare days or weeks worth of smoothies in advance by making smoothie bags. Chop all your smoothie ingredients and add them to individual freezer bags. In the morning, retrieve a bag from your freezer, dump it into the blender and add your liquid – no ice needed.

When In Doubt, Steam: There's nothing worse than feeling uninspired in the kitchen, but that doesn't mean you have to resort to cold, disappointing takeout. Whenever you're unarmed with a recipe or a plan, grab those vegetables and simply steam them. Finish them off with some olive oil and lemon juice, fresh herbs, or a thick and creamy tahini sauce and you're done! ! If you're someone who travels a lot or is on the go and hesitates to buy fresh produce, stock your freezer with frozen vegetables, which are perfect for preparing this way.

Cook in Batches: Prepare your beans and whole grains all at one time, store them, and then add them to your meals throughout the week. You can scoop them into salads and soups, make a breakfast porridge with the grains, or layer steamed vegetables in a bowl with beans and grains and top it off with a zesty sauce for an impromptu goddess bowl. You can even freeze any excess if you don't think you'll get to it all and then thaw it to use for the following week.

Make Your Own Salad Dressing

I never buy bottled salad dressings. They're full of sugar, emulsifiers and other fillers and preservatives. Instead I make my own. I usually mix up one of these two simple recipes, but you can create your own concoctions keeping this simple formula in mind: 60 percent oil (olive oil, avocado oil, walnut oil), 30 percent acid (lemon or vinegar), 10 percent accent flavors (Dijon mustard, garlic, ginger, tahini, tamari, herbs). You can play with the ratios to your taste.

PUT IT INTO ACTION

Which kitchen essentials do you have and which do you need? If you need to purchase anything, make a plan to do so or dust off anything you haven't used in a while and put it to work. As a bonus, you can also clean out your pantry, get rid of anything you haven't used or is expired, and add some of the fresh ingredients listed in this chapter.

Recipe: Everyday Lazy Salad Dressing

Ingredients

- ¼ cup olive oil
- Juice of half a lemon
- Sea salt and pepper to taste

Directions

1. Whisk and pour over salad

Recipe: Simple Vinaigrette

Ingredients

- ¼ cup olive oil
- 2 Tbsps. apple cider vinegar

- 1 tsp. Dijon mustard
- Black pepper to taste

Directions

1. Whisk and pour over salad

Chapter 12

Cook More with Less Stress

Usually when I start working with a client, she tells me that she doesn't cook because she doesn't know how, doesn't like it, or doesn't have time. Somewhere in the middle of our time together, this same client starts cooking.

To what do I owe this transformation? As a coach, it's my job to stretch people beyond their comfort zones. That's part of what drives the change, but I've come to realize that most women close themselves off to the idea of cooking before having all the facts straight, and therefore tend to stress about it unnecessarily.

Cooking for a dinner party of 20 can be stressful – I get it. But cooking at home for yourself or your family is not, and this is how to keep it stress-free.

1 – Keep it simple: It sounds cliché but the truth is that the simplest cooking methods like steaming, poaching, boiling, and en papillote (in parchment paper) are the best. They bring out the food's natural flavor and retain most of the nutrients. Learn these basic techniques and a delicious-tasting meal can be yours in minutes.

2 – Herbs are the icing on the cake: So you're steaming your heart out – did you know you can sprinkle some sea salt and pepper and drizzle some extra virgin olive oil on your meal and be good as gold? Clearly I learned this the long way around, so I'll save you some time: If you want to make your taste buds sing, really sing, add some fresh herbs – dill, thyme, rosemary, mint, cilantro – the possibilities are endless. Chop them up, sprinkle them on your fish, add them to your stir fry and blend them in your sauces. It works and it's impressive. That's all.

3 – Sauce is where it's at: We all crave comfort food and heartier flavors once in a while, so I hope you're paying attention because I'm about to give you a recipe for the only sauce you'll ever need. I pour this on anything, but mostly veggies and with the flick of a wrist instantly transform boring-ness into awesome-ness.

One of my clients named this Awesome Sauce and I have to agree that it is (p.s. – men will swoon and kids love it). You can find the recipe at the end of this chapter.

4 – Once you've mastered seasonings, eat with the seasons: This is so important. Basically, it means don't eat watermelon in December and butternut squash soup in August. Fruit and veggies taste better in season because they're fresh and haven't traveled around the world to get to you.

5 – Presentation is more than half of it: The eye informs the brain. Mario Batali wouldn't serve his pasta on paper plates and neither should you. Even if you're just starting out, be proud of your creations, use your best stuff, and arrange your food artfully on your plate. And if you've made something you're not crazy about, plate it up impressively and serve it with confidence. There. You just made it taste a whole lot better! Now smile and graciously accept those compliments!

6 – Color and Texture Count: This one's a little more advanced, but think about it like you would fashion. Mixing colors and textures like topping cooked food with raw garnish or crunchy veggies with creamy sauce adds depth of flavor and makes food more interesting. Nobody wants to eat a plate of food that is all one color or texture.

7 – No matter what you do, do it with love: I love dining out, but nine times out of ten, I like eating my own food a lot better. I'm no Rachel Ray, but when I'm creating recipes or making dinner at home with my husband, a lot of love and passion go into it. That's something you usually don't get in a restaurant. Even better, because cooking is so fulfilling to me, I find that I eat less and I don't feel bloated post-meal. I also get great leftovers for lunch the next day.

Even when I was new to cooking, burning my rice sucked, but I approached the learning process with an open mind and willingness to learn. So once I mastered the perfect rice, I felt an incredible sense of accomplishment. That same feeling – when I perfect a recipe or make something delicious – is what keeps me coming back to the kitchen. I still make mistakes, but I learn and move on.

I've found it helpful to think of cooking like shoe shopping– a means to an end to get that perfect pair of shoes. I don't know many women who don't love shoe shopping because it means the outcome is a beautiful, new pair of shoes that make you feel hot. So you might as well embrace the entire process – shopping, buying and wearing.

The same goes for cooking. I didn't always love the cooking process as much as I enjoyed eating a finished product. But, like shoe shopping, cooking has become one of my favorite pastimes.

What exactly makes cooking like shoe shopping?

1 – Inspiration: Whether I see a look in a fashion magazine that I want to recreate or stumble on a must-have pair of shoes on Pinterest, every great outfit starts with inspiration. Likewise, in cooking, inspiration comes from seeing a recipe that intrigues me on a blog, or picking up the season's best-looking squash at the Farmer's Market.

2 – Envision the Outcome: One of the most important steps in the process, but often overlooked, envisioning the outcome puts you closer to your goal. When I have an outfit in mind for a specific event or am dying for a pair of beautiful new shoes, I envision myself wearing them and how I'll look and feel. The same is true for cooking. I usually read and re-read the recipe, imagining myself performing each step and creating the finished product. If I want to change anything about the recipe, I think that through too. Just like you hang and organize your clothes neatly in a closet, your recipes deserve their own special storage to keep them organized and accessible, too.

If you spend a lot of time online, consider creating a Pinterest board to categorize your recipes or create a swipe file with book-marked links. You can access them easily on your phone, laptop or iPad when you need them. There's also an app called Paprika ($4.99) that makes it easy to copy recipes from the Web. If you prefer paper recipes, consider a tear file, album, or recipe box for keeping your recipes in one place.

3 – Assess the Situation: Of course, before any big purchase, I do the responsible thing and survey my closet to see if I already own a pair of shoes that will fit the bill. Aaannndd the answer is almost always No *(wink)*!

I do the same thing before I purchase recipe ingredients – take stock of my refrigerator and pantry to see what I already have on hand. If I have enough tahini, this saves me from buying another jar. And if the recipe calls for cilantro but I still have half a bunch of basil, you better believe I'm making a substitution.

Always use what you have to save on costs and minimize waste.

4 – Preparation: When I planned a surprise birthday party for my now-husband, I was so excited about the outfit I would wear that I laid out everything – from accessories to of course, shoes – on the bed hours before it was time to get ready. In cooking, this is called *mise en place* and it's crucial to recipe success. Making sure everything is pre-washed, chopped, sliced and measured minimizes mistakes and actually *saves* time.

5 – The Result: As women, we can all relate to those moments when we're wearing something that makes us feel our absolute best and it shows. Heads turn, compliments fly. Believe it or not, the same thing happens when I cook something I love and feel proud of (and that's a good thing because I spend more time these days in an apron than I do wearing high heels).

All this said, there is just one way cooking can't even compare to buying new shoes:

When you learn how to cook for yourself and eat well, your life starts to change and it brings more fulfillment than any pair of shoes, piece of clothing or of-the-moment handbag ever could.

PUT IT INTO ACTION

Use one of the recipes in this book or one you've wanted to try to cook a nutritious meal for yourself this week. Let go of the need to be perfect and just play and experiment in the kitchen.

Recipe: Awesome Sauce

Ingredients

- 1 inch ginger, peeled and diced
- 2 cloves garlic, peeled and diced
- 2 Tbsps. tamari
- 4 Tbsps.Tahini
- ½ tsp. maple syrup or brown rice syrup
- Juice of half a lemon
- Dash of cayenne

Directions

1. Blend all ingredients together adding water to get the right consistency. It will be creamy like a salad dressing and you can adjust the consistency to your taste by adding water.

2. Steam seasonal greens or veggies, combine with a cup of whole grains (optional) and drizzle with this savory sauce.

Chapter 13

Meal Planning in Minutes

There's a famous saying that goes "if you fail to prepare, you prepare to fail" – that couldn't be more true especially when it's applied to healthy eating. If you don't have your fridge stocked full of veggies and easily accessible snacks, it's going to be a lot easier to pick up the phone for takeout or swing by the drive-through on your way home from work. We want to avoid that at all costs.

In that case, meal planning is key, and this doesn't have to take hours on a weekend either. Here's my quick shortcut version of meal planning. However, don't be fooled. This still involves a commitment on your part and an investment in time that you may be spending elsewhere now. Assess where you can spend less time watching television or browsing the internet and where you can invest in planning and preparing some home-cooked meals for yourself. If it's important to you, you'll make it a priority.

First, spend some time browsing and brainstorming on Pinterest for inspiration. You can search different things like chicken or kale or vegetarian or gluten-free. Any keyword you'd like. Follow different Pinterest accounts that pin recipes you like and re-pin to your own boards to collect them. When you see a recipe that appeals to you as you browse the Internet or read blogs, pin it to your board. Make this an ongoing habit. If you don't use Pinterest, you can create bookmarks on your browser or even a paper file if you're more of a hands-on type. My mom stores her paper recipes in photo albums so they're easy to find and access. Recipe boxes are also cute but tend to fill up fast.

Then, each week choose a few different dinner recipes you'd like to try. Be sure they're simple. Avoid recipes with 20 ingredients and three hours of cooking time. Double the recipe if you need to so you can cook once and eat twice and plan to have the leftovers for lunch the next day or dinner the next night.

Make your shopping list with the ingredients and then go to the store or place a grocery order online!

Also during the meal planning stage, decide on 1 or 2 breakfasts for the week. You can prepare breakfasts in advance so they're ready to grab and go.

Think:

- Breakfast casseroles or egg muffins

- Overnight oats

- Chia seed pudding

- Pre-frozen smoothie bags

It's really that easy and it can also be fun.

Breakfast really *is* the most important meal of the day. For more breakfast ideas and recipes, download my 3-Minute Breakfast e-Book and downloadable meal planner at: http://bit.ly/HHTBookDownloads.

For those moments when you're uninspired, just steam some vegetables, dress them with a simple sauce like my Awesome Sauce (Recipe on p. 153), choose a protein and you're set.

What if you just don't have a plan or a list? I've still got you covered with my simple six-step process for power shopping for healthy meals. It's designed to get you into and out of the grocery store without getting distracted by all the extras that you don't want or need. You know how you can walk into the store for two things, become distracted and hundreds of dollars later leave with 17 items you never planned to buy? I call it the Target phenomenon. This is how you avoid it.

PUT IT INTO ACTION

Download the free meal planner and create a meal plan for this week. Print a copy for each week and get into the habit of doing this each week.

SUPERMARKET SWEEP
How to Power Shop for Healthy Meals with Marissa's Well-being and Health

GET EVERYTHING YOU NEED, EVEN IF YOU'RE SHORT ON TIME

DON'T LET TIME CONSTRAINTS KEEP YOU FROM EATING AT HOME. GET A FULL WEEK'S WORTH OF MEALS IN 30 MINUTES OR LESS

PRODUCE: Start here. This is where you should spend most of your time. Focus on leafy greens and choose 2-3 different kinds. If you're feeling adventurous, try something new!
If chopping intimidates you, choose pre-chopped greens and boxed or bagged, organic salad greens (baby spinach, baby kale, arugula).

OTHER PRODUCE: Grab 1-2 other colorful vegetables like carrots, beets, parsnips, squash. Look for what's in season or grown locally. Do the same with fruit.

Don't forget basics like garlic, onion, chilis, ginger and fresh herbs.

BULK BINS: Scoop up whole grains like quinoa or millet, dried beans or lentils and raw nuts.

DON'T FORGET YOUR EXTRAS:

TAMARI, BRAGG'S OR LIQUID AMINOS

NUT BUTTERS
OLIVE OIL
SPICES

EGGS
COCONUT OIL
MILK OR MILK ALTERNATIVES

CANNED GOODS: To save time, use BPA-free canned food like beans and wild caught salmon and tuna, all of which make fast additions to lunch-time salads.

SEAFOOD & LEAN PROTEIN: Look for wild and organic meat and seafood. Talk to your fish monger or butcher for recommendations. Stock up and freeze individually-wrapped pieces.

FREEZER: 1-2 bags of frozen fruit for smoothies. Keep frozen vegetables like corn, peas and spinach on hand to toss with whole grains. Also great for people who travel a lot and want a healthy meal in a pinch.

SHARE & PRINT:
Share on social media then save and take it with you to shop for a week's worth of healthy meals when you haven't planned ahead.

FAMILIES WHO EAT DINNER TOGETHER ARE HEALTHIER
People consume 50 percent more calories, fat and sodium when dining out, but that's not stopping most families. Percentage of meals eaten outside the home:

1960s 20% > 2010s 50%

TIME-SAVING TIPS FOR BUSY COOKS:
1. Wash and chop veggies when you get them home (or buy pre-chopped).

2. Cook pots of grains and beans and blanch vegetables all at once, then use them to create meals throughout the week.

3. Use slow cookers for meals you can cook once and eat 2-3 times.

4. Keep your most-used kitchen utensils within easy reach.

mwah!

MARISSA'S WELL-BEING AND HEALTH

www.MWAHonline.com

Download this image at http://bit.ly/HHTBookDownload

Chapter 14

The Daily Detox

We all have moments when we feel like we need to detox or clean out our systems, particularly after a weekend, a vacation, or crazy week of work travel. Instead of going on the juice cleanse roller-coaster, I recommend a few daily detoxifying practices that will eliminate that feeling and keep you refreshed on a regular basis – not just a few times a year. More than anything, these are just good self-care habits.

In the morning, upon waking and before eating breakfast or having coffee, prepare a morning elixir of hot (but not boiling) water and fresh squeezed lemon. You can add a tablespoon of apple cider vinegar, fresh grated ginger, and/or cayenne pepper. Drinking this will wake your digestive system, prepare your body for solid food, and stimulate your metabolism. This drink is also a great liver cleanser. It's like clearing the slate and starting fresh every morning.

Make sure you get a healthy dose of leafy greens each day either steamed, raw, in a smoothie or blended soup. Green vegetables are most often lacking in modern diets. Learning to cook and eat greens is essential to good health. Nourishing yourself with greens, naturally crowds out the foods that make you sick and sluggish. Greens help strengthen your blood and respiratory system, and the color green is associated with renewal, refreshment, and vital energy.

Nutritionally, greens are very high in calcium, magnesium, iron, potassium, phosphorous, zinc, and vitamins A, C, E and K. They're crammed with fiber, folic acid, chlorophyll and many other micronutrients and phyto-chemicals.

Some of the benefits from eating dark leafy greens include:

- Blood purification.

- Cancer prevention.

- Improved circulation.

- Strengthened immune system.

- Promotion of healthy intestinal flora.

- Promotion of subtle, light and flexible energy.

- Lifted spirit and elimination of depression.

- Improved liver, gall bladder, and kidney function.

- Cleared congestion, especially in lungs, by reducing mucus.

Avoiding toxins like sugar, caffeine, and alcohol can detox your system naturally. Try doing this for a few days at a time or even for a month to see how you feel. Always drink plenty of water to flush toxins from your system.

I can't tell you what a good sweat session can do to release toxins and give you a boost of energy. Break a sweat in your favorite exercise class, a steam room, sauna, or take an Epsom salt bath. A detox bath in Epsom salts, a combination of magnesium and sulfur, encourages the body to flush out toxins and has many more health benefits. Fill a bathtub of hot water with 2 cups of Epsom salt and a few drops of essential oil. Immerse your body in the water and soak for no longer than 20 minutes. You will sweat and notice your heart beating a little faster as it also promotes circulation.

Finally, twist regularly. Performing twists, as in yoga poses, compresses the internal organs to push out toxins from the blood. Those twists also promote circulation and healthy digestion.

PUT IT INTO ACTION
Make a habit of starting each day with hot lemon water.

Part 5

The Food-Mood Connection

Chapter 15

Listening to Your Body

Food offers a temporary reprieve from feeling. The tastes, the smells, the textures can transport us to a place where – temporarily – we don't have to feel anything but pleasure. Overcoming this means being able to listen to your body, letting yourself feel a range of emotions, having well-thought strategies for managing those emotions, and creating a new, healthier relationship with food through a combination of mindset and behavioral shifts.

The first step in this process is learning how to listen to your body to understand the hunger and fullness cues it gives.

You may not have ever considered listening to your body as an aspect of self-care, but it is. Managing what you allow into your body and how you treat it requires tuning into your body.

The phrase itself sounds a little cliché and the concept is certainly abstract. It's definitely not something we grew up learning how to do in school and it's certainly not often taught in health class.

This story illustrates what I mean by "listening to your body:"

It was the kind of fall weekend morning that was perfect for running: sunny and brisk. My husband and I had taken the subway from our downtown apartment all the way uptown to Central Park for a hilly run. It was early enough that the park was still quiet except for our fellow early-riser runners, cyclists, and walkers out with their dogs and babies.

I was fueled and hydrated and ready for an incredible run. But it was far from the run I anticipated. Because I'm active, whenever something is off – not enough sleep, I'm coming down with a cold, stress – I feel it in my body and fitness first. During this run, my breathing was labored, leg turnover slow, and my body felt heavy. I was depleted and I knew it, but I didn't want to admit it.

That particular summer, I had completed a triathlon and then gone on to start training for a half marathon. I had traveled to L.A. for five days, back to New York, and then back to San Francisco for a half-marathon all within the span of two weeks. Deadlines were piling up and I hardly had a moment to rest.

That day, my body knew I was run down, but my mind didn't want it to be. I had training runs to complete, but my body had other plans. Through the discomfort I experienced on that run – and several others like it in the days leading up to it – my body was speaking and it was my responsibility to listen.

Later that afternoon, after a nap and some food, I made the difficult but necessary decision to take several days off of exercise. Had

I not I listened to my body, I would have kept going and ignored all the signs that were telling me to slow down. But to what end? I may have gotten sick, injured or worse – collapsed – setting me back from my training and professional goals even further.

Everyone has a different threshold for how much they can handle on a physical and emotional level. *It's up to you to know yours.*

Listening to my body has been one of the best ways for me to get real about how I feel and what I need to be at my best.

It has successfully clued me in to which way of eating works best for me. After 20 years on a strictly vegetarian diet, I started eating seafood and eventually took away dairy. My body cued me on that. It's why I still eat whole grains when the rest of the world is eating Paleo. That's because my body tells me to, not the rules of any diet. And listening to my body is the reason I took a four-month running hiatus a few years ago against my own personal will.

Your body is like the quiet talker with the most important thing to say.

We live primarily in our heads and use our bodies as the vehicle to perform what our mind tells us to do. Getting out of your head and into your body means completely ignoring or drowning out the chatter in your mind and reprogramming old habits. If you live in your head as I often do, sometimes you have to stop or slow down and deliberately ask yourself what your body is saying.

Your body is like the quiet talker with the most important thing to say. Give it a turn to speak and listen hard when it does.

Listening to your body takes a lot of practice and, to be honest, it's not an easy skill to master. It's something I work on every day. Honoring my body and ignoring my head has been one of the most important aspects of creating true health in my life.

PUT IT INTO ACTION

Make a list of all the ways your body speaks to you and how you ignore it. What could you be doing differently to honor and listen to your body to give it what it needs?

Client Story: A Life Anchored in Food

During a session with Victoria, who was working on a 40-pound weight-loss goal, she had a breakthrough. We had covered what to eat and what to avoid, which foods were best for her body and which workouts motivated her to get to the gym. She got it. What she really needed to complete her weight-loss puzzle was to conquer her habit of emotional eating. I asked her about her upbringing and what mealtime was like in her house.

Proud of her Italian upbringing, she explained that mealtime was a social occasion; her mom made big meals for her and her brothers and they all sat around the table eating fast and talking about how good the food was. Even now that she had moved out of her parent's house, her mom still planned Victoria's visits home around what meals she would prepare.

Being 100 percent Italian myself, I could totally relate to this. As I listened to Victoria talk, I felt the love for her family pouring out of her. She had so much pride in her heritage and beautiful memories of mealtimes with her family.

But as heartwarming as it was, we also honed in on how it has shaped her own relationship toward food as an adult. Sharing those big homemade meals around the table with her family, Victoria came to associate food with love and comfort.

In her adult life, when she had a bad day at work or broke up with a boyfriend or felt any kind of uncomfortable emotion, Victoria would turn to food to dull the pain and call on that feeling of love that was missing in those difficult moments. This is common for anyone who overeats or struggles with emotional eating. Having a firm grasp on this, Victoria is now more mindful of the times when she is using food as comfort and we've worked on how to identify her triggers, counteract that habit, and form new ones in its place.

Chapter 16

Understanding the Crave Wave

Like many women, I used to think of cravings as the enemy. I would try to fight my cravings when they came on and think of them as a chance to exercise willpower.

Not anymore.

Many people view cravings as weakness, but really they're important messages from your body trying to tell you something. When you experience a craving, deconstruct it. Ask yourself, what does my body want and why? It's an opportunity to be honest with yourself about the eating habits, behaviors, and imbalance in your life that could be triggering those cravings.

Cravings – especially sugar cravings – are kind of a pain. On the one hand, we know we want to eat the best possible foods for our bodies, but on the other we have a little voice inside trying to tempt us otherwise, until we finally give in.

My years spent addicted to sugar and trying to fight it cold turkey got me nowhere. I've realized that to conquer any cravings, you have to first understand them – this is a much better strategy for learning how to deal with them, so let's start there.

Knowing why you may be experiencing a craving can help you pinpoint what's going on for you.

Some of the most common causes of cravings include an emotional response to being out of balance in some area of your life like career or relationships. Cravings can be due to a hormonal fluctuation, or a sign of dehydration, and of course most commonly cravings arise from low blood sugar.

When blood sugar drops too low, a subconscious fight-or-flight response is sent to our brains sending your body into a panic to eat, usually something sweet. If you have a diet high in sugar, processed foods and refined carbohydrates, chances are you have very poor blood sugar metabolism, which causes sharp and problematic fluctuations in blood sugar levels that trigger food cravings.

If you're aware of WHY you experience cravings, you can be better equipped to handle them.

When you feel a craving come on, deconstruct it. That is, instead of reaching for the food you're craving or even trying to ignore it, think first about why you're craving it.

Next, drink a glass of water and distract yourself with something else – a book, a walk, some other activity. Change your environment. If you're sitting at your desk, get up and walk around. If you're in your apartment, leave. Go do something else – take a walk, get a manicure, a massage or go see a movie.

If your craving still lingers, you *can* indulge it, but choose high-quality foods. For example, if you're craving chocolate, go for a piece of nice, decadent dark chocolate. Or if it's ice cream, try some really good full-fat, organic artisanal ice cream in a flavor you love. We tend to eat less of these high-quality foods because they're richer so they satisfy the craving better. Eat slowly for optimal enjoyment and really savor the flavor, the texture – every aspect of the food that is satisfying that craving.

Another option is to find a healthy alternative to nip the craving in the bud. For example, if you're jonesing for pizza, make your own healthy pizza and load it up with vegetables. If French fries are your vice, make some baked sweet potato fries. Blend frozen berries in your blender or food processor for a creamy treat as an alternative to ice cream. Get creative and soon enough you'll start to crave more of the healthy foods you love!

7 Simple Steps for Shaking Your Sugar Habit

I'll address some of the physical ways to break up with sugar in the next chapter, but there's always a mental component too. If you're still struggling with sugar addiction, try a few of these mental tricks.

Step 1: Change Your Mind

Instead of thinking of the craving as problematic or the enemy and hating yourself every time you slip up and eat a cookie, recognize that to your body and mind, sugar is a solution in the moment. This approach sets you up to successfully deconstruct the craving rather than feel like you're battling an evil demon. Be mindful that sugar is a way to get comfort, energy, or distraction. Feeling tired, sad, lonely, or unfulfilled can be quickly remedied with sugar – in the moment. But how can you fix those feelings long-term?

Step 2: Tune In

Now you're ready to deconstruct the craving. If you're accustomed to eating sugar regularly, you probably don't notice emotion tied to it. Start to tune in. When you feel a craving come on, take a deep breath and identify any feelings – physically, mentally, and emotionally. These are cues for why you're craving the sugar. Track those feelings in a journal. You'll notice a pattern with your cravings over time.

Step 3: Get Your Drink On

Before munching on a cookie or grabbing for the chocolate, drink an 8-ounce glass of water and wait 30 minutes. The craving may subside.

Step 4: Look Deeper

Cravings usually aren't about the food at all. If you're a sugar addict and water isn't working, determine where your life is sticky or out of whack. Do you have relationships that fulfill you? Do you have a career that you love? Is your spiritual practice nourishing? Do you move your body daily in a way that feels good to you? If any one of these is out of balance, you may be trying to fill a void with food.

Step 5: Envision a Sweet Life

What would your life look like if you could have everything you desire? How would you feel? How would you act? Spend some quiet time alone. Close your eyes and create an image in your mind. Then take time to journal about it. Set an intention around how you want to change your patterns both in life and around your cravings.

Step 6: Have a Backup Plan

Inevitably, you will have cravings and that's ok. Plan ahead and you'll meet them with ease and grace. Carry healthy snacks with you in your handbag or keep a stash in your desk drawer so the office doughnuts won't seduce you. There are plenty of recipes available for healthy substitutes that provide nutrition and use alternative sweeteners that won't send your blood sugar into a tailspin.

Step 7: Plan for Dessert

While I don't recommend dessert every day, once in a while the occasion calls for something sweet. On holidays, at family meals or celebrations, you may find it works for you to plan to eat some dessert – or whatever it is you crave. This keeps deprivation out of the equation and prevents gorging on sweet treats.

PUT IT INTO ACTION

Create a "nourishment menu," a list of activities you enjoy and that keep you feeling happy and fulfilled. Don't hold back. List everything you love to do, from making jewelry to dancing in your apartment. This is a self-awareness exercise. The next time you feel the urge to give in to a craving, look at your list and choose something else to do instead. The fulfillment you get from it will inevitably make the craving disappear. Try it and see what happens for you!

Chapter 17

Reversing the 'Sugar Shock'

Food, like drugs, alcohol, sex or gambling, has the potential to become addictive. A newborn's sense of taste is the most important and most-developed of the senses. According to the European Food Information Council, numerous studies show that across cultures, newborns show a strong preference for a sweet taste. This natural and innate association with sweetness and comfort follows us into our adult lives. It's no wonder we develop addictions to foods that taste good yet aren't necessarily good for our bodies. Sugar is one of those foods and it's one of the most addictive. Addictions allow us to attach to something in the absence of feeling safe.

Sugar is as addictive as drugs or caffeine and if you're a sugar-lover, you get it. Sugar is everywhere from your yogurt and cereal to tomato sauce and salad dressing. Manufacturers sneak sugar into their foods to keep them inexpensive to make and to get consumers dependent on them. If you're addicted to sugar, it's not your fault.

Many people live by the motto "everything in moderation," but with sugar that's impossible. Because it's as addictive as cocaine, it's impossible to stop at just a little. If you think about the times you're most likely to crave sugar, it's during the times of day where you most need energy – breakfast and snacks.

There are two main types of sugar – glucose and fructose. Many people erroneously believe that your body needs sugar for energy, but that's only partially true. Your body uses glucose, mostly found in vegetables and whole grains, for energy, not fructose. Healthy fats are another source of good energy. One of the best ways I've found to reduce sugar cravings is to eat more healthy fats in addition to adding nutrient-dense whole foods, especially plenty of fiber-rich vegetables and satiating protein. It's another case in which nutritious foods crowd out the less optimal sugary foods.

Quitting sugar cold-turkey can feel torturous without a backup plan. First, expect that your blood sugar will plummet – you may experience more hunger than usual and also extreme cravings. Know that for the first week or so, it will likely feel uncomfortable. Be with it and remind yourself that it's OK to feel uncomfortable. Remind yourself of the reasons why you're eliminating sugar and stay connected to them.

Have protein and fiber-rich foods at the ready like hard boiled eggs, rice cakes with nut butter, avocado or full-fat cheese with whole grain crackers (I like the brand Mary's Gone Crackers), full-fat yogurt or coconut yogurt with nuts and cinnamon, veggie crudité with hummus or black bean dip (homemade is best, otherwise check the label to ensure there is no sugar).

Having clear strategies to counteract any uncontrollable cravings that show up can also be a lifesaver.

For instance:

- Try a cheese plate instead of dessert.

- Sip licorice tea to fight post-meal sugar cravings.

- Skip the sugar in your coffee or tea.

- Take a teaspoon of coconut oil after or between meals

- When snacking on fruit, combine it with protein and fat (nuts or cheese) to reduce the insulin spike and slow down the absorption of sugar into the blood stream.

- Prepare healthier treats with alternatives like brown rice syrup or stevia for stand-ins when your cravings are at their worst.

When you've released sugar's hold on you, here's what you can look forward to:

- More satisfaction from your meals

- No more cravings

- Regulated appetite

- Sustained energy throughout the day without the mid-morning or afternoon slumps

- Clearer skin

- Better, more stable moods and more positive mindset

- A more peaceful relationship with food

PUT IT INTO ACTION

Get honest with yourself about the level of dependence you have on sugar. Think of one thing you'd like to try to limit your sugar consumption.

Chapter 18

Conscious Eating:
Fullness and Hunger

Do you ever catch yourself eating when you're not hungry, or do you more often than not eat so much you have to unbutton your pants?

When I was in college, my friends and I would often sneak off campus to the nearest Cheesecake Factory at our local mall. We would order their ample appetizers, larger-than-life entrees of pasta, pizza, burgers, and fries, and top it all off with a few shared slices of their dense cheesecake.

When I ate there, I didn't know when to stop. We left campus so infrequently and the food was so good (compared to campus food and to my unrefined palate), I would go crazy. There was no on/off switch on my hunger until it was too late. I left our dinners overstuffed and sick every time, without fail. But here's the rub: I accepted that sick and full feeling as normal, a regular side effect of going out to dinner. What I didn't understand then is that I could still enjoy my meal but learn to control how much I ate so I wouldn't feel that way.

Fast-forward five years while working in the corporate world. I had felt a tinge that I was meant to be doing something other than my 9-to-5, but what? I had no idea, so I just ignored that feeling and worked, partied, and shopped over it. At the same time, I started to have insatiable "hunger." "I'm *always* hungry," I would lament to my friends. I would snack for what felt like all day long every day on almonds, oatmeal, yogurt, cheese and crackers, you-name-it.

To no avail. The hunger remained.

What I didn't realize at the time was that the "hunger" I was feeling wasn't really hunger. There was an unfulfilled desire in me that I was attributing to hunger.

I was looking to food to fill a void that could only really be filled by looking inside myself and getting honest about what I really needed and wanted for my life.

This happens on a smaller scale in day-to-day life.

Stressed and on a deadline? Do you find you munch on chips? Annoyed with your boyfriend? Nothing a few happy-hour snacks can't cure. And so it goes ... Now that I've found my way, that insatiable "hunger" has subsided and I feel fuller than ever with passion for what I do and love in my life.

Hunger is controlled not only by the gastrointestinal tract (the stomach) but also by the hypothalamus (the brain). It takes your brain 20 minutes to receive the message that your stomach is full. So by the time you feel stuffed, it's already too late.

Now, whenever I'm hungry I play a little game with myself.

Instead of satisfying the "hunger" immediately, I check in with my body first and try to identify any emotions I'm feeling around the hunger or cravings, especially if I've already eaten a meal. My Conscious Eating Guidelines outline more tips on how to differentiate hunger from emotions like boredom, sadness, loneliness and stress.

Marissa's Conscious Eating Guidelines

- Stop and breathe.

- Before you reach for the snack, ask, "am I *really* hungry, or am I bored, tired, sad, lonely, happy, some other emotion?"

- Identify where you're feeling the hunger (stomach, head, heart, chest, mouth.) Hint: if the hunger isn't in your stomach, it's likely another emotion driving feelings of hunger.

- Answer the question, "if I couldn't have food right now, what else would I need?" A nap? A hug? A manicure? A good cry? Ok, go get it! If you can't take a nap or cry at the moment, take a 5-minute walk, or make a note to go to sleep earlier or phone your mom or a good friend later on and let it all out.

- Drink an 8-ounce glass of water and wait 30 minutes. Thirst and dehydration often show up as hunger.

- If the desire to eat goes away, you were likely experiencing emotional hunger. If the desire to eat intensifies or you want to eat foods that are normally unappealing to you, you're hungry. Go eat already!

I want to share with you some tools that I use with clients in my health coaching practice that can make tuning into your body much easier and more mindful. The hunger fullness scale, which you can use while you're eating, guides you to eat until you're 80 percent full (or at 8 on the scale).

The 80 percent theory is based on the Japanese concept of Hara Hachi Bu, a rule borrowed from the Okinawan diet of eating until you're 80 percent full. It can help with weight loss and also makes digestion a lot easier on your body. Okinawans live the longest and are the healthiest people on the planet, so I'll take a page from their book any day!

Looking more closely at the hunger fullness scale, you can see all the different stages of hunger and fullness. We've all been in each stage at some point in our lives. Take some time to think through what each stage feels like for you. When do you or have you experienced each stage?

I'm happy to say that now I never allow myself to get to the point of fullness I did in my Cheesecake Factory days. What helps me is checking in with myself while I'm eating, asking myself where I am on the scale. As it says, we want to work toward eating in the grey areas: starting when hunger awakens, at a level 3 or 4, and finish at completely satisfied (level 6, 7 or 8) to help balance blood sugar and manage portion sizes.

Trust yourself to let go of portion size expectations and experiment with intuitive eating using this scale as a guide. Once you get used to working with it, it will become second nature. If you often find yourself eating too much at mealtime, or eating to the point of feeling bloated and over-full like I did in my Cheesecake

Factory days, thinking of hunger and fullness on a continuum is the best guide for knowing when to eat and when to stop.

The Hunger-Fullness Scale

Hunger / Full		
	0	Empty
	1	Ravenous
	2	Over-hungry
	3	Hunger pangs
	4	Hunger awakens
	5	Neutral
	6	Just satisfied
	7	Fully satisfied
	8	Full
	9	Stuffed
	10	Sick

Source: Diettogo.com

The next table is a comparison of physical hunger vs. emotional hunger. This can be a useful tool to identify when you're actually hungry versus when something emotional is triggering your cravings and appetite. Again, just something to be aware of right now and if you can, start identifying moments of emotional eating if you're prone to it. Like breaking any habit, awareness is the first step.

Physical Hunger		Emotional Hunger
Tends to come on gradually and can be postponed	VS	Feels sudden and urgent
Can be satisfied with any number of foods	VS	Causes very specific cravings (say, for pizza or ice cream)
Once full, you're likely to stop eating	VS	You tend to eat more than you normally would
Doesn't cause feelings of guilt	VS	Can cause guilt afterwards

Source: Sanfordhealth.org

As you eat, practice slowing down, checking in with your body to see how you're feeling, and tuning into where those edges are for you.

It takes practice, but the more mindful you are, the more your body will thank you. Imagine leaving your home or restaurant after a meal feeling like your spunky, energetic self with enough energy to go dancing instead of wanting to go home and go to bed!

PUT IT INTO ACTION

Work with the hunger and fullness scale to cue you on when to eat and how to know when to stop eating.

Part 6

Beyond Food

Chapter 19

Changing Your Relationship with Food

Healthy eating isn't about "good" vs. "bad" or "success" vs. "failure." There's no virtue in eating 100 percent vegan or Paleo or raw or anything else. Don't put those burdens on yourself. A way of eating doesn't define your self-worth. Get comfortable enough with yourself to know what makes you feel your best and what your body needs and wants, then eat to support your Highest Self as often as possible. If you fall off the wagon, guess what? You're human. Tomorrow's a new day. There's beauty and righteousness in all imperfection.

> There's beauty and righteousness in all imperfection.

Changing your relationship with food isn't an easy thing to do and it doesn't happen overnight. Throughout this book I've probably challenged your current perspective a lot. That's by design. I want you to be curious and dig deep to understand your own relationship with food, where it came from and how you'd like it to evolve.

Your current habits, thoughts and beliefs are deep-rooted in your past experiences. You may have heard your mother or older sister speak unkindly about her own body when you were growing up, or someone may have commented on your physical appearance or specific behaviors. Maybe as a teenager you saw a commercial or TV or magazine ad that stuck with you and affected you in a way you didn't realize until now.

In my own case, I was teased in elementary school about my bad, broken-out, adolescent skin, and my prominent nose, and this had a much bigger impact on my self-worth than I ever realized. My grades and my petite frame were the two things that got me the most attention so that's where my value and focus lied. I could study and focus on maintaining my weight. This mindset followed me into my adult life.

When I graduated from college and started working full-time, my busy lifestyle as an urban professional left me little time to cook. Eating was never about nourishment. Instead, I grazed so I wouldn't eat too much. My grab-and-go meals like pizza on my way to class or macaroni and cheese out of the pan, weren't healthy choices, but I didn't know any better. Besides, I never ate enough of anything for it to matter, or so I thought.

One day, a conversation with a friend at the gym turned to nutrition and I realized just how sub-optimal mine was. Almost immediately, I became interested in cleaning up my diet. Within a few months of eating mostly whole foods, I realized how much better I looked and felt.

Ironically, being cleaner on the inside gave me more confidence and mental clarity and something in me started to shift; I felt an innate sense that I was meant to be doing more meaningful work in this world. With a stable job, a good salary and a shiny new Master's degree, I was scared to admit it – or even tell anyone. Besides, what else could there be?

The feeling persisted for almost five years as I became more and more stifled, uninspired and unhappy in Corporate America. It's no coincidence that during that time, despite my healthier new way of eating, I developed a sugar addiction and affinity for binge drinking.

Through a lot of self-exploration and chance meetings, I discovered health coaching and knew I had found my calling, but fear paralyzed me from taking immediate action. Almost five years later, I enrolled in a health coach training program. As a Health Coach, the work I do gives me purpose and put me on a path to finally feeling whole.

As a result of finding my purpose, the rest of my life fell into place. I started my blog and launched my health coaching business, I started dating the man who is now my husband, and I developed a much healthier relationship with food.

Eating became about nourishment, and I realized just how physically and emotionally damaging my drinking binges were and eventually, they too, became a thing of the past. My reliance on sugar even started to subside. It would take a lot more work on myself and more learning about nutrition to get where I am now, but it was a start.

Meanwhile, the more I became immersed in health coaching and owning a business, the more disconnected I became from my corporate job. With a plan in place, I began working toward a goal of leaving that corporate job, and when it felt right, I did. At the time, it was scary and there were lots of uncertainties, but looking back, it was the best decision I've ever made for my health.

One powerful strategy for changing my relationship with food as I changed my diet was food journaling. Studies show that when trying to lose weight, those who keep food journals are more successful than those who don't. That's because food journals keep you accountable, bring awareness to your eating patterns, and also help you discover which foods are best for you.

Some people are hesitant to keep a food journal at first because they think it makes them too fixated on what they're eating. But that's not the point of food journaling the Holistically Hot way. Instead of journaling for calorie counts and macronutrients, use a food journal as a way to stay accountable for what you choose to eat, and also to determine how food makes you feel, both physically and emotionally. If you're always hungry an hour after your lunchtime salad, maybe it's time to consider a different meal. If you get a headache every day at 3 p.m., your food journal can clue you in to the foods, behaviors, or deficits that may be the cause.

Every meal is a new opportunity to make a healthy choice.

A word about grazing: The unhealthy choices aside, my grazing was a problem in and of itself. Grazing is common in women who come to my coaching practice. Some aren't educated about how to build a healthy plate, others are afraid of committing to the calories of a full meal. Let's call it like it is, though. Grazing is mindless eating and not only can it lead to eventual weight gain, you also don't get to experience full satisfaction from food.

First, when you graze all day, by the end of the day, you may end up eating more than you would have had you just sat down to your meals mindfully, throughout the day. Also, grazing doesn't necessarily result in feeling satisfied, hence the need to constantly try to find something else to eat. Finally, grazing has an emotional element to it and is actually not really driven by physical hunger but rather emotional hunger resulting from stress, boredom, or sadness.

> **If we're ever going to heal our relationship with food, we have to stop treating it like the enemy.**

Regardless of what food noise you experience, let go of whatever negative thoughts you have about what and how you ate yesterday and just be good to yourself today.

Every meal is a new opportunity to make a healthy choice.

And if all else fails, breathe, start again, and be thankful for all that you have.

If we're ever going to heal our relationship with food, we have to stop treating it like the enemy.

Becoming Mindful

I was an awkward-looking teenager. My dark hair, prominent nose and bad skin in a sea of blonde hair, blue eyes and button noses in my southern hometown of Louisville, Ky., meant my self-image took a blow during my formative years.

I wasn't happy with my appearance, but by high school I realized that, since I wasn't conventionally pretty, my grades could get me the positive attention I craved. So I focused on studying to make grades that would get me into my first-choice journalism school, Northwestern University. It was the first time I understood the concept of controlling outcomes. It was this time in my life when I developed a Type A personality which would shape my adult life.

In adulthood, that Type A personality wasn't as productive for me as it was in high school. I have a laundry list of ways that being controlling in this way failed me, from doomed relationships to impossible-to-tackle "to-do" lists. Mindfulness wasn't a part of my vocabulary and eventually it knocked me down hard. In trying to control the direction of my life, my exercise, my relationships, my drinking, my eating all very much became out of control. There was no mindfulness in any of it.

In your passion, you'll find your purpose.

My yearning for a more purposeful life that I had ignored for many years finally called out to me loud and clear. My transformation into becoming a Health Coach led me to a more mindful way of living. For the first time, I could take a step back and more clearly than ever see the damage my choices were doing to my mind and body.

The moment I let go of trying to control my life and instead let myself be guided by what was in my heart was the instant that everything changed. By embracing and nurturing my passion, I found my purpose and myself.

In your passion, you'll find your purpose.

I truly believe that when you find yourself and discover what makes you come alive, the damaging behaviors and thought patterns that keep you stuck naturally fall away, without even trying.

PUT IT INTO ACTION

Start a food journal to help you understand your relationship with food and how you can be more mindful about eating. Do you struggle with emotional eating? Is your daily afternoon snack making you feel tired or giving you a headache? A food journal can help you understand your patterns.

Client Story: Inspired to Do What I Love

Charlotte had just graduated from college and was new to New York City. Her new consulting job was fine, but was sort of like trying to fit a round peg into a square hole. Blogging was a favorite pastime and photography was her true love.

She was a stunning beauty with a strong physical presence, but when we met for our sessions, Charlotte was quiet and reserved. I struggled to pull her out of her shell. We worked on making some basic changes to her eating habits and she implemented them well, but she had a strong emotional connection to bread that we traced back to her childhood being at home in her mother's kitchen.

As we worked together, Charlotte came out of her shell as she made some even bigger changes in her life – moving back to her hometown, enrolling in photography school, and accepting a job as an apprentice with a professional photographer.

Not only was she able to put down the bread, she eventually went gluten-free after discovering a severe intolerance to gluten and wheat.

Here's what Charlotte had to say:

"Perhaps the biggest thing I took away from working with a Health Coach might not have been anything related to diet or exercise. Marissa helped me see how important it is to do what I love, surround myself with people I care about and set aside time for myself. I found that the times when I was doing the things I love: photography, blog design, reading, painting, blogging, etc., I felt more fulfilled and in turn, thought a lot less about food and exercise."

And that shell I mentioned? Years later it's completely gone! She even agreed to record a video testimonial of our work together!

This story also is a good example of how cravings and attachments to certain foods can be a sign of a food intolerance, which was true in this case.

Chapter 20

Upgrade Your Day

Since nutrition is so central to this book, it's important to address how eating can and should be an act of self-care, especially with the "food as fuel" approach to eating.

It's absolutely imperative that you put the best, highest-quality foods in your body to provide your fuel. That's ultimately what it's all about.

There is no end to the limiting mindsets that keep us stuck.

Being healthy is not equivalent to being perfect.

Another one that I run into a lot with clients – and even *I* used to think this way – is that you have to be perfect to be healthy.

That's certainly not the case at all. You don't have to be die-hard about healthy food. For example, if you ate healthy all week and want to have some French fries on the weekend, then go for it.

Being healthy is not equivalent to being perfect. This is one of those subtle mindset shifts that make a huge difference when you finally start to believe it. Healthy eating is about being mindful of the whole of your diet, not obsessing about individual portions.

Healthy living isn't about being perfect and eating perfect. If you have the knowledge you need, feel in tune with your body, and trust yourself to make good choices, you will – and you'll do it consistently.

> **Healthy living isn't about being perfect and eating perfect. If you have the knowledge you need, feel in tune with your body and trust yourself to make good choices, you will — and you'll do it consistently.**

Perfect is not sustainable and doesn't exist. Let's focus on the "p word" – progress – instead.

The truth is, you can make simple upgrades to your daily habits that will drastically improve your well-being. You can start small and then build on these over time.

When I work with clients in my health coaching practice, instead of eliminating foods or habits right off the bat, we talk about how we can upgrade them. It takes some of the pressure off and makes the prospect of change seem less jarring.

These are just a handful of simple ways to upgrade your day:

Cooking | Play with your food: You know that eating nutritious food is a crucial part of taking care of yourself, but take it a step further. So often when we prepare our food we plop it onto a plate or eat it directly out of the paper takeout container because we're in a rush. Try plating your food nicely, then sitting down to it at a table with a nice place setting and maybe even a candle. You'll change your entire dining experience this way.

Showering | Brush yourself dry: I've tried the latest skin treatments and enough lotions and potions to make your head spin. But nothing compares to dry brushing, a method of stimulating the skin using a hand-held, stiff-bristled brush or mitt to improve circulation and appearance. Before you shower, take two minutes to use a dry brush to brighten and naturally detoxify your skin. It's also invigorating! The rigid bristles of the brush stimulate below the surface of the skin to get blood flowing and promote healthy circulation. A dry brush typically costs $7-$10.

Once you have the brush of your choice, start at your feet and make upward sweeping movements along your legs, thighs, buttocks, abdomen, arms, shoulders, chest and back. The whole process takes two to three minutes. Do it daily for the best results.

Sleeping | Rest easier: Diffuse essential oil in your bedroom while you sleep. My favorite is lavender. It calms you down so you can get a deeper, more restful sleep.

Dental Hygiene | Scrape your tongue: Sounds gross, but keep reading. Tongue scraping is not only cleansing, but also stimulating and it goes that extra mile toward fighting plaque and keeping your breath fresh. It supposedly enhances kissing, too!

A tongue scraper is a metal U-shaped tool you can find at a health food store or Amazon. It's used to remove excess bacteria and food build-up from the surface of the tongue. With the rounded edge of the tongue scraper, apply light pressure and scrape down the tongue with a few quick strokes. Rinse the tool under water and continue to scrape until any white residue is gone. Do this two to three times per day, after brushing. You can buy a tongue scraper for around $5 -$7 at your local health food store.

A tongue scraper is the best way I've found to make my visits to the dentist more enjoyable. When I first saw this U-shaped, stainless steel utensil, I was perplexed and a little scared. It turns out it's the best way to keep plaque at bay.

You may have heard of oil pulling, an Ayurvedic self-care practice of swirling coconut oil around in your mouth. Some of the benefits of oil pulling include detoxification, teeth whitening, reduced bacteria in the mouth, and less inflammation in the gums, and fresher breath.

Most oil pulling how-to's online recommend swishing a tablespoon of coconut oil around in your mouth each morning on an empty stomach for 20 minutes or longer. You can definitely try this if you have the time. However, for those who are short on time or cannot stomach a mouthful of oil, you can still reap many of the benefits by using coconut oil as a moisturizer after brushing.

This recommendation comes from my dental hygienist Karl Dixon at Tribeca Center for Integrative Holistic Dentistry. Put a small amount of coconut oil on your toothbrush and spread it strategically around the periphery of the mouth, focusing on the front and back of the gums and teeth and all the hard-to-reach nooks and crannies. Rinse your toothbrush and spit any excess coconut oil in a tissue and discard it in the trash (spitting in the sink could clog the drain). Do this twice a day after brushing.

Midday Recharge | Sip a Hot Beverage: Trade the coffee for your favorite hot tea or even hot water. Sipping plain hot water is hydrating, detoxifying, and gives your immune and digestive systems a little boost. More gentle than coffee, tea is calming and can help curb those afternoon sugar cravings. Take 15-30 minutes out of your day to recharge and for an added bonus, stay off your phone and computer.

Nighttime Relaxation | Face or Hair Mask: Shut down the computer and give yourself some extra TLC with an extra-special beauty treatment like a face or hair mask. Pair it with a soak in a hot tub of Epsom salt and essential oil for maximum relaxation. Epsom salt can be found at any pharmacy and has several health benefits when you dissolve two cups in a bath of warm or hot water. It can ease muscle tension, treat colds and congestion, detoxify, and just relieve stress. Soak in an Epsom salt bath for 15 to 20 minutes and you're sure to feel relaxed. Epsom salt promotes circulation so don't be alarmed if you notice an elevated heart rate and even sweating when bathing. This is normal and it's why it's not recommended or necessary to soak for prolonged periods of time.

Daily Calendaring | Say Yes Less: Most of us are over-scheduled. Make it a practice to give yourself more time by eliminating engagements that aren't necessary or re-prioritizing them for a later date.

Write It Out | Journaling: One of my clients used to get anxiety right before bedtime — so much so that she couldn't fall asleep. She would mentally run through everything on her to-do list right when her head hit the pillow and, not surprisingly, it would cause her insomnia. I recommended a nightly practice of journaling and guess what? She started sleeping like a baby. Getting your thoughts out on paper can make a drastic difference in how you process information and deal with emotions. Many people feel lighter and some people even experience weight loss as a result.

If nighttime journaling doesn't speak to you, you can journal in the morning, a la Julia Cameron's The Artist's Way. She recommends stream-of-consciousness writing to fill three sides of paper first thing every morning. You can write about anything you desire, the idea being to get everything off your chest before the ego passes judgment, which can lead to inspiring and life-changing breakthroughs.

Take-It-Anywhere | Deep Breathing: Regular mindful breathing is both calming and energizing. It clears the mind and reduces stress. You can incorporate deep breathing into your regular meditation practice or do it separately. There are several breathing exercises to choose from. I recommend a 5-5-7 breath. Breathe in for five, hold for five and exhale for a count of 7. Repeat up to 10 times. You can literally take it anywhere. Mindful breathing works instantly to calm you down by tricking your brain into thinking you're relaxed.

Indulging | Cook for Your Cravings: If takeout and restaurants are your weakness, make your favorite foods at home and upgrade the ingredients. Try pancakes with coconut flour, buckwheat flour or almond meal or Pad Thai with spaghetti squash or zucchini noodles. You get all the flavor of your favorite foods with more nutrition and none of the salt, sugar and additives found in prepared food.

PUT IT INTO ACTION

How can you implement simple upgrades into your life? Don't try to do everything at once. Choose one thing that appeals most and try it for two weeks. Then build on that foundation and add another.

How to Make Healthy a Habit

The key to creating healthy habits is not as complicated as it may seem. You may have heard that it takes 30 days to form a habit, but that's based on hearsay. Scientific research shows that it takes anywhere from 18 to 254 days to create a habit.[19]

Science aside, the best way to create a habit is to practice the habit you'd like to cultivate – maybe it's morning exercise, meditation, journaling, drinking warm lemon water every morning – it could be anything. The key is to keep practicing it consistently and set out to do it for 30 days straight.

There will be times during those 30 days when you won't want to do it. Force yourself to do it anyway. If you miss a day, just get back on track the next.

The idea is that you keep practicing it until the feeling and experience you create by doing it is one you can't imagine living without. Creating healthy habits allows you to create a proverbial "shelf" full of practices that you can rely on when you need them.

---

[19]   http://www.huffingtonpost.com/james-clear/forming-new-habits_b_5104807.html

Recipe: Healthy Pad Thai

Ingredients

- 1 small spaghetti squash (1.5 to 2 pounds)
- Juice of 1 lemon
- 1 ½ Tbsps. mirin (a rice wine vinegar)
- 1 ½ Tbsps. fish sauce
- ½ jalapeno, minced
- 1 Tbsp. water
- 1 Tbsp. grape seed oil
- 3 cups thinly sliced mustard greens (or any other leafy green)
- 1 14-ounce container extra-firm tofu, cut into 1/4-inch cubes, (or you can sub with and equal amount of chicken)
- 4 large eggs, whisked
- Peanuts, chopped, or you may use cashews

- Cucumber, chopped

- Pea shoots

Directions

1. Preheat the oven to 375 degrees. Slice squash in half length-wise, scoop out seeds and prick the skin all over with a knife. Coat flesh with oil and roast on a rimmed baking sheet about 1 hour, or until tender when pierced.

2. Whisk together lemon juice, mirin, teriyaki sauce, jalapeno and water in a small saucepan. Bring to a simmer; keep warm over low heat, whisking occasionally.

3. Heat oil in a large skillet over medium-high heat; add greens and sauté 1 minute. Stir in tofu or chicken if you're using it, and cook, stirring occasionally, 3 minutes (cooking time will be slightly longer for chicken). Reduce heat to low and pour in eggs. Let sit 30 seconds, then stir constantly until eggs are just cooked, about 2 minutes more. Turn off heat.

4. Using a fork, scrape squash from shell. Transfer strands to skillet and fold into egg mixture. Drizzle with sauce, stirring to incorporate. Garnish with peanuts, cucumber and pea shoots.

Chapter 21

Sustainable Self-Care

Aside from going to the gym every day, I used to do little else to take care of myself. I gave 200 percent to my job and my guy-of-the-moment, but rarely did anything for me. It's no wonder I was rewarding myself with Pinkberry and chocolate chip cookies!

Does this sound like you? Then hop on the self-care train for a few of my favorite ways to show myself some TLC and they don't require a ton of time – or money.

Here's the deal: You can be super-healthy eating all the right foods, exercising and more. But if you're not taking care of yourself, it'll only get you so far. All of the nutrition stuff just doesn't translate without self-care.

People often say to me, *"but Marissa, I have a family/job/social life that needs me, I don't have the money for regular, luxurious massages or I don't have the time or patience to sit and meditate for an hour."*

The idea that self-care has to be time-consuming, expensive, or even selfish is completely out of the question because it doesn't. There are plenty of ways that self-care can be sustainable – meaning you'll be able to stick with it, prioritize it and actually look forward to it.

Most importantly, the idea that self-care is selfish is a lack mindset that keeps us stuck in old behaviors. As women, we're caregivers by nature, so the concept of actually putting ourselves before someone else seems counterintuitive or even wrong.

The reality is that before you can take care of the others in your life who need you most, you have to take care of yourself. The example that's often used is the airline safety best practice of putting on your own oxygen mask before helping younger children with theirs.

Get into the practice of checking in and asking yourself every day what you need most. Some days it may just be 30 minutes of silence with a cup of tea before the kids wake up. Others, it may be an entire afternoon of "you" time. Just remember that YOU deserve everything you give to others.

Sipping Hot Water

Even the healthiest among us can feel less than our best at times. You know to drink more water, but instead of gulping it down cold, try sipping your water hot.

If you have pesky health problems like PMS, joint and muscle pain, or belly bloat, then a groggy lymph system may be to blame.

Your lymph system is kind of like you. When you're stressed and tired, you don't do your best work and neither does your lymph system. Sipping plain hot water is a simple way to fully rehydrate, detoxify and pep up that lymph to stimulate weight loss, improve digestion and fortify your immune system.

Invest in a thermos and keep it full of hot water to sip throughout the day. Make sure your hot water is as clean and pure as your cold drinking water.

Meditation Made Easy

One of my goals is to be more consistent with my meditation practice. The one thing that has made the most difference is taking a meditation-made-easy approach.

Meditation makes life a little better. Answers come more readily, days flow more easily, emotions feel more grounded. Everyone can use some meditation in their lives, which is why I always recommend it to clients. Yet it's often met with trepidation.

Why? Because it *seems* like an intimidating thing. A lot of people shy away from meditation because they think it has to look like this: sitting cross-legged on a pillow chanting for hours on end. Not one bit! Meditation can be exactly what you make it. Thirty seconds, three minutes or three hours – it's all meditation! A regular practice can help clear your mind and change your perspectives.

These are a few of my meditation-made-easy tips that can make the practice more approachable:

- **Keep it short – faster than a polish change.** Even if it's just 5 minutes a day, it's still meditation and you still get the benefits. You can always build up to longer sessions once you get used to it.

- **Find guided meditations that you like on iTunes.** Having someone talk you through it at first can be comforting and helpful. You can find guided meditations online. Gabrielle Bernstein has a collection of guided meditations also on iTunes, most of which are less than 10 minutes. Also check out apps like Head Space that make meditation more approachable.

- **Be Patient.** I'm often told that when someone "tries" to meditate they find their minds wandering, even racing. So they give up. Of course your mind will race, especially when you're new to meditating. That's expected. Just notice it and clear your head. Then keep going. As many times as necessary. Most importantly, don't judge yourself when this happens. With practice, you'll improve.

- **Make it a ritual.** To keep myself on track, I've built meditation into a morning ritual. I wake up earlier than necessary so I can have some time alone. I prepare my morning detox drink and then I meditate and write in my journal before my workout. This process takes me no more than 30 minutes but makes a major difference in my day. If I skip it one day, things feel a little "off."

Meditating at the same time every day makes it a regular habit. You might want to start or end your day with it, couple it with your morning tea or evening journaling. When you make it habitual like this, you'll enjoy it more because it's not just another item on your to-do list and you'll actually stick with it.

Like anything else, if you have to go searching for it, it's less likely to happen. I keep my guided meditations organized in a playlist and upload them to my phone. You can use Spotify or iTunes for this. This way, I can get to them easily no matter where I am. In case you can't squeeze some time in at home, you can get to it on the subway, in the carpool line, or on an airplane.

You might even consider carving out a special place in your home where you meditate. Have everything you need right there so you can get right into it. This might include a special pillow, some spiritual items like crystals or mala beads, candles or incense, or even a blanket.

Remember that meditation is a practice. Keep going with it, be as consistent as possible and it will get easier, become enjoyable, and create noticeable changes in you and your life.

Sweet Sleep

Sleep is not a luxury; it's a necessity. And if you're not getting enough, you should start making it a priority to get as much as you need and can get.

And just how much is that? Everyone is different but around 7-9 hours a night is recommended by The National Sleep Foundation. Sleep is the sacred time when your body repairs itself from all the days' activities. It's also when the nutrients from your food go to work for you. Night owls take heed, because the hours between 10 p.m. and 2 a.m. are crucial. This is the timeframe when the most regenerative sleep happens so you definitely want to be resting during then.

You can set yourself up for the best quality sleep by making your bedroom a sanctuary conducive to sleeping – keep it dark, cool and relaxing – and try to limit screen time before bed.

On this same token, give yourself some down time during the week as you need it. I used to be out every night networking and socializing, but I realized that doesn't work for me anymore. I'm much happier and more energetic and productive when I have regular down time to recharge.

Aside from green smoothies and healthy food, sleep is right up there on my list of favorite things. I crave it and I know my body needs at least eight hours of it. Unfortunately, in our hectic lives, sleep is one of the first things to go.

Trying to get more done in a day, we sacrifice sleep. Someone once said to me that "sleep is free so why wouldn't you take all you can get?" That really stuck with me.

Here are my tips for how to get more and better quality sleep:

1 – Power Down: Turn off the computer, television and other electronics at least one hour before you go to sleep. This helps to quiet the mind chatter and de-stimulate the senses.

2 – Set the Mood: Put yourself in the mood to sleep by playing relaxing music, taking a hot soak in the tub, lighting a candle, and doing some deep breathing or meditating.

3 – Create an Oasis: Clear your space of all clutter and have clean sheets. I also like to diffuse lavender essential oil.

4 – Stop Sipping: Stop drinking liquids around 6 p.m. Part of sleeping well is making sure your rest is uninterrupted and getting up to use the bathroom doesn't help.

5 – Cut the Caffeine: Similarly, lay off any caffeine after 3 or 4 p.m.

6 – Power Nap: Although it's not always feasible, if you can do it, take a 20-minute nap daily to recharge your battery.

7 – Give Yourself a Bedtime: My bedtime is 10 p.m., and while I don't make it to bed at that time every night (I do most nights), it gives me a time to work toward so that I'm controlling my evening and it's not controlling me. If I didn't have that time in mind, I would hang out on my computer a lot longer or channel surf all night.

When you're well-rested, you keep your blood pressure and cholesterol in check, reduce stress levels, have more energy, stay more alert and think more clearly, increase immunity, and experience fewer cravings and a more predictable appetite.

Basically, you can get *more* done in a day and *feel better* all day long when you have *enough sleep.*

PUT IT INTO ACTION

Almost everyone can use more sleep. Give yourself a bedtime and hold yourself to it. If you've got sleep covered, how else can you be taking better care of yourself? Stress is one of the most common causes of heart disease, weight gain, and acidity/illness in the body. What can you do to relive stress in your life and put yourself first?

Client Story: A 'People Pleaser'

Danielle was a people-pleaser and emotional eater. She had been giving to everyone else her entire life and it made her feel good. But when she came to me, she knew something had to change and thought it was her diet.

Yes, there were aspects of her diet that needed to change, but what she discovered by working with me is that she actually needed to do a lot more to care for herself. We worked on simple ways she could say 'yes' to herself and when she began to practice some of these simple acts of self-care, she noticed that she relied on food less to soothe her.

It's no surprise to me that investing more in taking care of herself was the lifestyle change Danielle needed to make to change her relationship with food and turn around her emotional eating tendencies.

Chapter 22

Exercise & Movement

While we've been focused on food for most of this book, there's more than just food that contributes to a healthy body and, of course, exercise is on that list. I have just two guidelines when it comes to exercise. 1) Do what you love and 2) be consistent. When you master the first, the second will naturally follow.

I can't tell you the number of women who tell me they despise running but feel like they "need to" or "should" do it either because they've read it's good exercise or everyone they know is doing it. To be consistent at something and to get the benefit of it, you have to want to do it. This applies to anything – beyond exercise.

If you're forcing yourself to do something you don't love or that feels painful to you – physically or mentally – you're exercising wrong. Yes, you should challenge yourself, but if your chosen form of exercise doesn't feel fun, inspiring or satisfying, find something that does. If not, you risk injury, burnout, and a lack of results.

Exercise is healthy. There's no doubt about it. But as fitness gains momentum with trendy workouts and inspirational messages, is it possible that we're overdoing it? Could less be more? Should you exercise less?

In most big cities across the country, there's certainly no dearth of high-intensity classes and trendy fitness studios challenging us with heavier weights and faster sprints.

I love exercise and I love these classes – but not every day.

With all the endorphins you get from exercise, it's easy to overtrain to addiction. I know because I once suffered from exercise addiction myself, hitting the gym as much as twice a day most days.

While I don't discourage exercise, I feel it's important to shine a light on the reality that it's possible to exercise too much and too hard.

When clients who "eat well and exercise regularly" complain they're unable to lose weight, one of the first things I consider is the possibility of overtraining.

I don't mean to say that everyone needs to tone it down or cut back, but if you're putting in high-intensity work every day or even most days, you may be doing your body more harm than good. Chris Kesser, an expert in functional and integrative medicine, says less is more if you're someone who has an existing autoimmune disease, problems with your gut or adrenal fatigue.

You might be familiar with research showing that shorter, more intense workouts are more beneficial than hours-long, steady state cardio.

That is, if you're smart about it and don't overdo it, according to a recent controversial study published in the February 2015 issue of the Journal of the American College of Cardiology. The study found that slow jogging is more beneficial than fast running. [20]

Intense overtraining, or extreme physical stress, activates the release of cortisol, a stress hormone. It works the same with mental stress, too. The body perceives intense exercise as stress, cortisol is released at sustained levels consistently over time, and that results in any of a long list of issues from depression to weight gain and digestive problems.

Overtraining also impacts your immune system. Kresser calls this immune system "hyperactivity" – cellular damage during overtraining which can lead to autoimmune disorders.[21]

Finally, there's the possibility of something more dangerous like rhabdomyolysis, a serious condition that needs immediate medical attention when exercise breaks down muscle tissue. In some cases, that muscle protein is released into the bloodstream and damages the kidneys. My dad, an emergency medical physician, says he's seen an increase in "rhabdo" in the ER in recent years.

---

20   http://well.blogs.nytimes.com/2015/02/04/
      slow-runners-come-out-ahead/?_r=2
21   http://chriskresser.com/why-you-may-need-to-exercise-less/

If you experience muscle pain and swelling or brownish red urine, this could be a sign of something more serious and you should see a doctor immediately.

Some common signs you're generally overtraining, include:

- fatigue or a general feeling of exhaustion
- frequent colds
- muscle loss or weight gain

The best remedy for overtraining is rest. Listen to your body before your mind and reduce the frequency of intense training. Not every workout has to be all-out. Take a dance class, practice yoga, go on a walk. Find ways to make movement feel luxurious and enjoyable too.

PUT IT INTO ACTION

Decide on some exercise that you enjoy, then determine how often you'll do it. Schedule your workouts in your calendar, just as you do a doctor's appointment or important meeting. You'll be more likely to stick to it.

HIIT WORKOUTS

Personal Trainer Cindy Lai of Cindy Lai Fitness, who shares the same exercise philosophy, offers this done-for-you, take-it-anywhere HIIT workout you can do at the gym or at home.

Why HIIT (High Intensity Interval Training)?

- Burn more fat in less time with better results
- Build lean muscle and boost your metabolism
- Increase strength and endurance effectively

30 Seconds On/ 30 Seconds Off.

Choose 5 of the below exercises using compound movements (several muscle groups at once), set a timer, and go all-out during the working portion.

Do 2-3 rounds and rest 1 minute in between sets. This should take 5-17 minutes depending on the number of rounds. Do these intervals 1-2 times a week and mix it up. You can also do shorter or longer intervals.

- Jumping jacks
- Squats
- Pushups
- Burpees
- Planks
- Mountain climbers
- Dips
- Lunges

Cindy Lai Fitness www.cindylaifitness.com

CINDY LAI
FITNESS

BOOT CAMP | PERSONAL TRAINING | KETTLEBELLS

Chapter 23

Conscious Living

Conscious living is something else to consider within the context of healthy living. I'm certain that if, as a world, we lived more consciously, our lives would flow better, there'd be less war and more love and kindness.

Conscious living is bringing the awareness you have about your body and health to the outside world through compassion, mindfulness, aligned thoughts and desires, and not just going through the motions as can often happen.

When you're practicing living more consciously, you'll notice your life shift in even the subtlest ways.

Set aside time to regularly reflect through journaling, prayer and meditation. This allows time for thoughts and feelings to flow through you. We move through life at such a fast pace that we often don't give ourselves time to be and feel. And on that note, yes, it's ok to feel your emotions and not ignore or breeze over them.

Set goals once or twice a year or set smaller goals more frequently. Setting goals is the best way I know to stay focused, feel accomplished, and stay connected to a bigger vision.

Take a regular inventory of relationships, career, finances, and how you spend your free time. Things change and shift in any given year – or even month – so you'll always have an opportunity to see where you are and reflect on where there are any imbalances and what you can do to correct them.

Get in the habit of thinking about how your choices and behaviors impact the world. How can you make more-sustainable food choices? Some may choose not to eat meat, others may want to eat locally and seasonally and support local farming. Think about how much waste you create and where you can cut back, compost and recycle. Even something as simple as turning off the lights when you leave a room to conserve energy will make a difference. All of these choices impact the greater good in some way.

Finally, many of us accumulate a lot of excess stuff. I know I'm guilty of this, but it's something I am actively working to improve. Excess things can weigh us down in ways we don't realize. I try to be mindful now about buying things I don't need, and a few times a year, I clean out closets and drawers to free up space and give to charity or sell old clothes and accessories. When you do this, you cultivate a feeling of lightness and give to those in need.

PUT IT INTO ACTION

How can you live more consciously and practice mindfulness in your daily life? Will you make more sustainable food choices or think twice about buying things you don't need? I recommend starting with a closet cleanout to cultivate a feeling of lightness and signal a fresh start.

Part 7

Real Life Application

Chapter 24

Dining Out

D ining out when trying to transition to a healthier way of eating can cause anxiety because suddenly you're not in control of your meal. That's ok. You don't always have to be 100 percent in control to get a healthy meal when you know these healthy dining tips, which will help you order with ease.

First, you can ask to substitute things. Don't be shy about it or ashamed, it's totally fine. Salad for French fries is a good trade so is spinach or broccoli instead of a baked potato. If you have special dietary requirements, let your server know. Most restaurants expect patrons to have these needs and a good server will help you navigate the menu to find something suitable and to your liking.

Check out the energy of the place where you're eating. I used to get a salad from a busy deli salad bar every day for lunch. I always felt rushed when I was ordering; the guys who made the salad were frantic and banged things around. They rarely listened to my order and I often left feeling frazzled. The energy of those making the salad and how it was made didn't feel right to me.

I even began to notice I didn't feel well after eating those salads despite what seemed like a bowl full of healthy ingredients. So I stopped going to that place for salad. Be an energy detective and assess the energy around the food establishment to decide if it's someplace you want to eat. We absorb the energy of the food we eat.

Most restaurant portions are HUGE! I always draw an invisible line down my plate and eat until that point, checking in to assess how I feel along the way using the hunger and fullness scale. Once I eat to that line, or even before, if I feel full, I'll stop, put down my fork and ask for the rest to go. If I'm still hungry, I keep eating. But I always repeatedly check in as I eat.

On that note, you don't always have to order the entrees. Consider one or two appetizers instead, or an appetizer and a side. The leafy greens tend to be in these sections of the menu, so always look to order something green. And to combat those large portions, consider sharing an appetizer and an entrée with someone else you're dining with. The meals are often enough for two and you may find you're plenty satisfied.

Likewise, don't feel confined to exactly what's on the menu. If you see an ingredient as part of another dish, chances are that ingredient exists in the kitchen. Ask for it prepared your way – steamed, grilled, or sautéed to your liking.

Order your food dry, which is another way of saying without too much oil or butter. Healthy fats are fine, but some restaurants don't use high-quality ingredients and others don't use healthy portions of them – a lot of restaurant food is drenched in butter and oil. The same goes for salt. You can also request for your food to be prepared "light on the salt."

If you wake up feeling off after a meal out, don't beat yourself up. Drink some hot water with lemon and get back on track the next day with a healthy meal full of leafy greens, protein and healthy fat.

Social Life & Romantic Relationships

I'm often asked what to do about relationships, especially romantic relationships where one partner eats healthier than the other. This is not a reason to stress out, abandon your efforts, or make it a deal-breaker for the relationship. Instead, use it as an opportunity to set an example. Do your healthy thing and you may notice your partner wanting what you have. Healthy choices are contagious. This happened in my own relationship. When I started to make kale salad, the first few times my husband – then-boyfriend – skipped over it. Now he requests it.

Focus on making healthy food taste good. Nobody will turn down delicious food. You can make healthier versions of your partner's favorite foods, too. This is how I developed my recipe for Healthier French Toast recipe found in my 3 Minute Breakfasts eBook, which you can download at http://bit.ly/HHTBookDownloads

If you often feel influenced by your partner's choices, have an honest discussion and let your partner know how important a healthy lifestyle is to you. Opening up the line of communication is key and something we often dismiss.

Sometimes you will have to compromise. If they have a favorite restaurant they want to go to on a special occasion, be kind and go. Use the restaurant tips here to help get you through it.

Overall, put yourself first and do what you need to do to stay committed. It may seem selfish, but looking after your health is not selfish. You're all you've got in this one lifetime. In the long run, you're not only helping yourself but your partner too.

Despite your best efforts, you may find that there are people in your life who are negative and try to derail your healthy habits. So what do you do in those situations? Here's what I've found works over the years.

Be forgiving: It may sound far-fetched, but the best way to counter negative reactions to your new lifestyle is to respond with kindness. If you're experiencing teasing or friends and family who challenge your healthy decisions, recognize (inside) that their reaction may be based on their own fears – perhaps they've wanted to make similar changes but don't know how or aren't ready yet. Say a prayer wishing them happiness and stay focused on your own positive changes.

Give a Little: Sometimes all it takes for friends and family to understand your decisions is to invite them over to your side – just for a night. Offer to have them over for dinner, organize a potluck where you can cook up and share some of your own healthy creations, or invite them to your favorite healthy restaurant.

Letting others into your world gives them a taste of what you're up to and shows them that being healthy can be fun and delicious.

It goes both ways. My husband eats the way I do 90 percent of the time, so once in a while, I'll make one of his favorite recipes for chicken or pork. I don't love the idea of preparing meat, but it makes him happy, so it makes me happy. I keep it healthy and usually adapt one portion of it to make a version of the meal for myself without the meat.

Create New Rituals: There are times when new lifestyles require new friends and new activities. Find friends who share your beliefs and enjoy doing the same things you do – sharing recipes and health tips and engaging in healthy activities. You know the old saying, "make new friends and keep the old?" Now is a good time to put it into practice.

Be Gentle: Being forceful or militant in your beliefs never worked for anyone. Understand that there's room for everyone in this world. *Just be you* and treat everyone as your equal wherever they may be on their own journey. The more those around you see your glow from the inside out, the more interest they'll take in what you're all about.

Educate and Believe in Yourself: Know what you're doing and why, and do whatever it takes to get there. Read, work with a coach, take a class. I caution anyone who adopts dietary changes because they're trendy. Determine if and how this lifestyle will work for you – and only you. If you're eliminating whole food groups, know how you'll supplement the nutrients those foods provide and how it's benefitting your health. The more you know about your new chosen lifestyle and the more you believe in yourself, the more respect you'll gain.

Travel

Travel can be another tricky situation. One client who was doing really well with healthy eating on her home turf, but when it came to traveling for work she didn't exercise the same health-mindedness. There were a lot of things at play here, which we worked through together. But the main issue was that she just wasn't prepared on the road the same way she felt prepared at home. Whether you're traveling for business or pleasure, it's important not to not be too stringent and allow yourself some flexibility, but also not to throw caution to the wind.

However, airplane food and hotel breakfasts are no excuse for derailing your healthy eating plans, and you can keep your eating consistent, energy levels up, and your weight down while on the road.

Take snacks that travel: Stash snacks in your carry-on to munch. Things like raw nuts and seeds, dried fruit, baby carrots, a bag of frozen edamame which will thaw by the time you board the plane, whole grain, gluten-free crackers, a travel-size package of nut butter, or homemade granola bars all travel well and will make it past airport security.

Pack your own food: An apple and trail mix may be the obvious choices, but you can take it up a notch and bring food you can rely on for an impromptu meal. What you can't take in your carry-on, pack in your suitcase for when you reach your destination. A green salad in a to-go container, a ripe avocado to slice on top, and pre-cut lemon wedges to use as salad dressing (you may be able to score a small container of olive oil from a restaurant once past security) makes for a meal better than airplane food.

Hydrate: Purchase a large bottle of water to drink while on board your flight or bring your own bottle to fill from an airport water fountain.

Don't go hungry: Try to eat a healthy meal before you leave for the airport so you don't arrive absolutely starving. With snacks in tow (as per above), you should be able to make it to your destination unscathed by airport food.

Get creative: Even the most unimpressive of airports has a newsstand that sells snacks. If you're absolutely stuck, choose the best options there like trail mix, almonds or veggie crudités in a pinch.

Ask nicely: If you're staying in a hotel, politely explain your special needs. You may be able to score blenders, hot plates or even a mini-fridge to store snacks and meals with very little trouble.

Preparing for travel can be time-consuming, but keeping the above items on hand means that you can prepare food for your trip in a matter of minutes. You may even wish to research your destination in advance to find markets and healthy restaurants you can visit when you arrive.

PUT IT INTO ACTION

All of these healthy living tips, tricks and insights are no good if you can't apply them in the real world. The best thing to do is go out and live your life and practice using them yourself.

Not the End, the Beginning

Now that we're nearing the end of the book, what happens when it's over?

Before we part ways, I want to prepare you to feel confident that you can handle anything life throws your way with this newfound knowledge you have. Remember that you're never alone. Revisit this book as often as you like and you can join the private Facebook group, **Holistically Hot Women**, a community of women on their own health and wellness journeys, for extra support. I encourage you to get involved in the discussion forums there at: https://www. facebook.com/groups/holisticallyhotwomen.

One basic rule I want you to always remember is that life is for living. You are not here to be perfect. There will be vacation, you might get the flu, you will have too much to drink, or eat something or many somethings you wish you hadn't. It's ok. Do not panic.

The best thing to do – what I do – is reset with whole foods. Many people will react by jumping into a juice cleanse or going on a crash diet. Not you. You don't need that. What you'll find more often than not is your body will tell you when it's time to reset by craving greens, veggies, fruit and lots of good-for-you foods. Listen and give your body what it needs.

If you're interested in reinforcing some of the concepts in this book, join me for one of my group coaching programs or consider working with me in my 28-day jumpstart or 90-day intensive.

Always take things one day at a time and be realistic about what you're capable of in the moment. If you can only do one thing that day, do that one thing and don't judge yourself for it.

Of course, always keep in mind that living a healthy life is not about living a life of deprivation. Not even for a second!

Making any kind of change in your life can feel overwhelming.

If you're ready to make positive changes to your health and well-being but the very thought of it sends you into a frenzy, start small.

Choose one or two small things you know you can do that will make a positive impact on your health.

- Use salad plates for your meal instead of dinner plates.

- Aim to eat leafy greens at every meal.

- Increase your water intake by one glass a day and build from there.

- Take the stairs instead of the elevator or get off one stop earlier on the bus or subway.

- Move your body for at least 30 minutes a day.

Small changes add up to big shifts. The most important thing is that you start somewhere!

Final Word

Many coaching clients come to me wanting to lose weight – often the last five or ten pounds.

I frequently get detailed emails from women desperate to "lean out," counting macros down to the milligram and "eating clean" to exhaustion, frustrated that nothing has happened.

I totally know the feeling.

I felt this way most of my life. If I was just a few pounds thinner, then it seemed like all the missing pieces of my life's puzzle would fall into place. Everything would be <u>exactly as I wanted it to be.</u>

I'd weigh myself every single day hoping those last few pounds had disappeared.

They never did.

I'd run a marathon! That would be the ticket to my coveted goal weight.

It wasn't.

I exercised daily and ate healthy.

I didn't get it until I got it.

It all kind of happened at once, but eventually I stopped caring.

I got busy launching a career in health coaching and fell in love with a hobby-turned-career.

I saw myself with a purpose to be of service and fell in love with me.

I was effortlessly dating someone (the man who is now my husband) who saw past all my flaws and I fell in love with him.

And my weight? Suddenly, it could wait.

I've learned that if you want to lose the weight, you have to stop obsessing.

> ... about the number on the scale.

> ... about every last morsel of food you put in your mouth.

> ... about being perfect.

Why does obsessing counteract your efforts?

Your body's typical reaction to stress is a fight-or-flight response that raises hormone levels. The process is self-regulating, so once the stress is gone, hormone levels go back to normal.

I've learned that if you want to lose the weight, you have to stop obsessing.

But .... chronic stress (yes, this includes constant worry about what you're eating *and* too many grueling workouts) plus all the typical everyday stressors like work, family, and relationships will keep those hormone levels elevated for a prolonged period of time.

The result? Your body will hang right on to that weight.

I hope reading this book has given you an arsenal of practical tips you can apply to your life or creating lasting healthy habits.

But if you only take one lesson from these pages, I hope that you:

Live more.

Laugh more.

Love more.

And trust that everything will be as it should.

xo, Marissa

sunday	monday	tuesday	wednesday	thursday	friday	saturday
Create a wellness vision to kick off your month of health. **01**	Choose an ingredient from the top 10 list and google an easy recipe to make with it **02**	Try a new fitness or yoga class. **03**	Grab a journal and make some notes about your cravings. Any patterns? **04**	Smile at a stranger. **05**	Make a nourishment menu to use when a craving strikes. Unleash your creativity and decorate it. **06**	Take a mini-break with a cup of tea. **07**
How are you doing in the areas of: + Relationships + Career + Exercise + Spirituality Choose 1 that's out of whack and make a game plan to improve it. **08**	Choose a green smoothie from the Bonus recipes and enjoy! **09**	Connect with a friend or family member over the phone or in person instead of sending an email. **10**	Make a clean sweep with a tongue scraper. **11**	Eliminate sugar, gluten or restaurant fare for a week or even a few days and see what happens. **12**	Choose one new smoothie from the Bonus section to make every day for the next five days. **13**	Plan your reward for your completion of these 30 days. A few ideas: + A vacation + A massage + A mani/pedi + A new pair of shoes **14**
Add a probiotic to your daily routine (either natural or a supplement) to ease digestion. **15**	Sip some hot water. **16**	Make a small investment in a stiff-bristle brush and try dry brushing your way to glowing skin. **17**	Adopt your own personal mantra. **18**	Drink a green juice. Never had one? Go to your nearest juice bar and ask for all greens with apple, lemon and ginger (optional). **19**	Remember to stretch after every workout. Do a few extra minutes of stretching today. **20**	Try a sea veggie today. Find them in the Asian food section of your grocery store. Many have recipes right on the package! **21**
Do some deep breathing or meditation. Head over to iTunes to download a free guided meditation. **22**	Try one of the healthy tips for dining out. **23**	Clear your living space of clutter – choose a closet or a drawer. **24**	Eat breakfast! **25**	Try coconut oil in your cooking. It's great for sautéing veggies. **26**	Are you drinking enough water? Aim for half your body weight in ounces – daily. **27**	Celebrate yourself today! **28**
Catch some good Zzzs tonight. Aim for 7-8 hours. **29**	*Nice work!* Create a calendar like this for next month. **30**					

Marissa's Well-Being and Health *mwah!*

About the Author

Angelica Glass Photography

Marissa Vicario is an award-wining, board-certified Integrative Health and Nutrition Coach, blogger, and Women's Healthy Lifestyle Expert. As the Founder of Marissa's Well-being and Health, she is passionate about teaching women to trust themselves to make nutritious, slimming, and energizing choices without resorting to fad diets and all-juice cleanses. Her tips, recipes, and expertise have been featured on The Dr. Oz Show, The New York Times, Entrepreneur Magazine, Glamour, and Next Generation TV among many other women's lifestyle publications. When she's not teaching workshops and cooking classes or coaching clients in her private or group programs, you can find her traveling with her husband, David, running with the New York Road Runners or experimenting with flavorful, healthy recipes.

Work with Marissa

Support and accountability are proven to make all the difference when reaching your goals and they're two key ingredients I can't offer in a book.

If you wish to work with me to reach your health and wellness goals in a way that's fun and fearless, visit my web site at **www.MWAHonline.com** to learn more about my private and group coaching services.

If you're ready to get clarity around your goals and discover what might be in your way of reaching them by way of an action plan, book your complimentary 30-minute Freedom From Fad Diets Breakthrough phone session with me at http://bit.ly/HHBreakthrough.

Speaking & Events

Interested in having Marissa speak at your organization, conference or event?

Her corporate wellness and speaking experience includes audiences as big as several thousand to as small as ten at conferences, schools, events, and organizations like:

- Pfizer
- The Healthy Living Summit
- Claudia Chan's S.H.E. Summit Week
- Next Generation Start-ups Conference by Next Generation TV
- Tranquil Waters The ELEVATE Series: Workshops for Women
- Lululemon
- Athleta
- International law firm Skadden, Arps, Slate, Meagher & Flom
- Chaise Fitness
- Spa Finder Wellness HQ
- Channel V Media
- The Institute for Integrative Nutrition
- Young Female Entrepreneurs of NYC
- The New York Junior League
- One Medical Group
- New York University
- Chi Omega Collegiate Chapters and Alumnae Groups

She can speak on the following topics and many more:

- Green Your Diet and Cultivate Healthy Habits that Last
- Shake Your Sugar Habit
- How to Make Healthy a Habit
- Nutrition for the Road Warrior
- Sustainable Self-care

Health Coaching

This book was inspired by my experience at the Institute for Integrative Nutrition® (IIN) where I received my training in holistic wellness and health coaching.

IIN offers a truly comprehensive Health Coach Training Program that invites students to deeply explore the things that are most nourishing to them. From the physical aspects of nutrition and eating wholesome foods that work best for each individual person, to the concept of Primary Food – the idea that everything in life including our spirituality, career, relationships, and fitness contribute to our inner and outer health - IIN helped me reach optimal health and balance.

This inner journey unleashed the passion that compelled me to share what I've learned and inspire others.

Beyond personal health, IIN offers training in health coaching, as well as business and marketing training. Students who choose to pursue this field professionally complete the program and are equipped with the communication skills and branding knowledge they need to create a fulfilling career encouraging and supporting others to reach their own health goals.

From renowned wellness experts as Visiting Teachers to the convenience of their online learning platform, this school has changed my life and I believe it will do the same for you. I invite you to learn more about the Institute for Integrative Nutrition and explore how the Health Coach Training Program can help you transform your life.

Feel free to contact me to hear more about my personal experience at Marissa@MWAHonline.com, **http://bit.ly/ BecomeIINHealthCoach**, or call (844) 315-8546 to learn more.

Angelica Glass Photography

Share the Love

If you liked this book, please visit the sales page on Amazon to leave a review.

For more about Marissa and this book, visit **www.MWAHonline. com/HolisticallyHotTransformation.**

APR 1 3 2017

CPSIA information can be obtained
at www.ICGtesting.com
Printed in the USA
LVOW11s2008200317

527832LV00003B/303/P

"This book captured me right away and I found it very relatable."

— **April P., New York City**

"Marissa's personal stories made it easy to relate to her as I read and as someone not familiar with the field of nutrition, she organized and explained large amounts of information in a way that was easy to understand."

— **Jennifer B., New York City**

"An enjoyable read."

— **Alisa W., Alexandria, Virginia**

"Marissa is a lovely combo of coach, knowledgeable nutritionist, cheerleader and she took an unshakable stand for my health, getting me to think about food and my own habits around it in a new light. She's also funny and relatable, which put me at ease to open up. She never judged – just listened, heard me and gently but firmly guided me back on the right path, never letting me get away with my usual ways of talking myself out of doing something. I'd recommend her to anyone who wants to revolutionize their way of approaching food."

— **Joanne W., Brooklyn, N.Y.**

"Marissa has a soul that sets her apart from other coaches in her field. She changed my life."

— **Laurel, L. Hoboken, N.J.**

"Your Holistically Hot Transformation is written by Marissa Vicario, a graduate of the Institute for Integrative Nutrition, where she completed a cutting edge curriculum in nutrition and health coaching taught by the world's leading experts in health and wellness. I recommend you read this book and be in touch with Marissa to see how she can help you successfully achieve your goals."

— **Joshua Rosenthal, MScEd, Founder/Director,**
Institute for Integrative Nutrition